Body Language

How to Analyze and Read People Better

By Sally Stephens

Copyright @2019

If you like my book, please leave a review. I would appreciate it a lot. Thanks!

Table of Contents

Nonverbal communication has always fascinated people. We have always wanted to comprehend the message behind the words; we have always would like to know what people actually mean by a look, a blush or a gesture.

Now we have realized not only that we can use nonverbal communication to translate other people's actions, but that we can also use it to give ourselves increased efficiency in life. Now body talk can help us prosper in life, in love and at work.

Human entities have probably always known naturally that our non-verbal communication is just as vital as our verbal communication. How many of us were told when young to 'stand up straight since our those with kids realized that would make us look more intelligent, attractive or excellent. Now research has shown that if we modify the way we present ourselves to the world-with good friends, at work and in love we stand a much greater chance of success.

This book explains how to improve your nonverbal communication, and the specially commissioned illustrations show you what works and what does not It encourages you to analyze and translate others' body language so that you can tell beforehand how to respond to them, and after that adjust your own body language for optimal impact.

If your aim is to get the most out of life, then what you really need is 'body language.' The study of body language-the art of non-verbal communication-- is possibly the most amazing and beneficial development in individual psychology today. It adds a whole new dimension to what you can comprehend about people and a whole new set of possibilities as to what you can achieve in the world.

People use several channels of communication. Yet, despite countless years of human development, we have concerned only the verbal channels as important-- what we say and what we write. It's only throughout the last forty years or so that we have realized that there's a whole channel-- non-verbal communication that is just as crucial as words, because it gives us just as much, if not more, information about what people are thinking and feeling. Some estimates suggest that up to 93 percent of the information we receive about any circumstance comes non-verbally rather than verbally. So, whenever you talk with a friend, ask your boss for a raise or set out to seduce, what you do may depend on thirteen times as information-packed as what you say.

Mind-reading

Body movement not only gives you additional info about other people and about yourself, it also gives you different information While people's words tell you only what they consciously really want you to know, their body language tells you an entire variety of other things, much of which they might not know they're exposing, and even understand themselves. People's fundamental character, the role they're playing the feelings they feel, the direction of their thoughts, their relationships with others-- not to mention what they actually think about you-body language communicates everything. And whereas people's words can hide a wide variety of tricks, their body language is a lot more hard to fake.

Similarly, naturally, your own body language will whether you like it or not-transmit information about yourself to others. And research studies have revealed that what you 'say' non-verbally is often far more prominent than what you say verbally, not only since it bypasses the mindful mind of a listener and speaks straight to his or her subconscious, but also because people rather appropriately trust non-verbal messages more than they trust words. The bad news is that your nonverbal communication is making declarations about you all the time, and some of these may be things you are attempting to hide. The bright side is that properly and genuinely used, body language can mention what you could not perhaps say out loud, in a way that actually reaches other individuals. I am competent ... I really need your support ...! like you. I love you.'

Body language isn't only about communication, however. What psychologists have realized over the past decennium is that if you change your nonverbal communication, you can actually change all kinds of things about your approach to life. You can, for example, modify your state of mind before going to a party, develop a better feeling towards your partner or feel more confident at work. And, obviously, if your nonverbal communication really shifts, and you connect differently with people around you, then they in turn will respond differently to you-so that the way you predict yourself to others will be shown back to you, in a cool circular process.

Words of warning

Because nonverbal communication is such an effective tool, you need to take care when using it. So, before you begin, a few words of caution!

First, it's a misconception that nonverbal communication allows you to read a person like a book. This theory. which was an attempt to 'alphabetize' non-verbal communication by specifying a single gesture as having a single meaning, was initially fashionable in the sixties. If people scratched their noses, that meant they were lying. It didn't matter whether they were scratching because their nose itched, as they were anxious or because nose-scratching was a crucial routine in their subculture-they were still seen as lying. Nowadays, we know it's just not that simple. Body movement aspects differ in meaning, and can be understood only in the context of a person's life situation.

Second, using body language successfully isn't about neglecting the words. Though we people are apes- and a lot of the body language series we use come straight from those developed by apes-- we are nevertheless talking apes. Therefore, much of this book is about using nonverbal communication together with the words, to highlight them, to elaborate on them, to control them or even to oppose them. To be a real body language professional, use your non-verbal abilities in addition to, not instead of, your verbal ones.

Finally, do not think you can use body language to get others to do what you really want. People aren't fools. If you try using non-verbal techniques so as to manipulate a person into liking you then naturally they will respond to what you do - but they are going to also respond far more highly to those of your actions that expose your control. They'll sign up, typically automatically, your incorrect smile, your moving eyes, your nervous stutter-- and will act accordingly. So if you're expecting to be able to rule the world through body language, you're going to be disappointed.

Practice makes perfect

How can you best usage body language? The first step is to develop your powers of observation, collecting as much knowledge as possible when you interact with others. Looking is the most apparent way and probably the channel through which you are going to acquire most information. Listen, too, not so much to individuals' real words but to the way those words are said, the way voices sound as people speak. Your other three senses, touch, odor and taste, can also tell you an unexpected amount: the heat and moisture of an associate's handshake can give you important clues regarding how positive he is about the meeting, a good friend's body odor will actually shift if she ends up being frightened throughout a scary film; a lover's taste will change as he ends up being aroused.

As you be more expert, you will be able to see not only the more obvious macro-clues, such as people's gestures or facial expressions. You'll also have the ability to identify the much more subtle and even more fascinating 'micro clues.' So, although in the beginning you might spot only the macro clue of a person's upset clenched fist, in time you are going to also register the micro-clue of their skin color change when they just begin feeling inflamed. With practice, your proficiency of micro-clues will let you understand - and even anticipate - just how those around you are thinking and feeling, and so be one step ahead all the time.

Pay attention to your own body language, too: you yourself are a major source of info, Screen your external signs, noticing how, as you respond to what's happening, your body position changes, your movements adjust your voice changes, your breathing shifts. Monitor, too, the internal signals that only you are actually aware of the butterflies in your stomach that tell you you're excited, the tension headache that notifies you to stress, the internal image of your lover's face when you think of him, the internal noise of a friend's voice when you imagine speaking with her. These are vital signs of what your body is telling you.

To know just what to watch out for, you really need a body movement vocabulary. The following are the necessary aspects of this, the ones on which this book is based:

LOOK: Look at an individual's height, their natural skin, hair and eye color, their body shape. Within the limitations of plastic surgery and the camouflage of outfits, all these things can tell you precisely what a person's gender is, their age. racial background and culture.

STYLE AND IMAGE: Notice outfits, hairdo, makeup, accessories. These generally show you short-lived things, such as age, the fashion sub-culture with which a person recognizes, their status in society, what type of job they have and their leisure interests.

POSTURE: Notice particularly the way a person stands, how they arrange their body, the angle at which they hold their body and head, and the direction in which their arms and legs are pointing. These aspects cannot only give clues to permanent things such as upbringing and age. but can also expose passing thoughts and feelings, specifically interest respect and approval.

GESTURE AND MOVEMENT: These are particularly important when used with words, highlighting and including emotional markers' to speech, rather like the punctuation marks that can give additional meaning to written words. Everyone may well also have a customized set of gestures he or she regularly uses-look specifically at upper body and limb movements, gestures of hands and feet, and head nods and shakes.

FACIAL EXPRESSION: Irreversible facial lines developed in time tell us about personality, notice the 'strive' wrinkles between a person's eyebrows, or the small, inward mouth lines that signify a keeping' personality. Also crucial are short lived facial expressions such as frowns, which show you how a person thinks, feels and relates moment to moment.

EYE MOTION: We give and get more information from the eyes than from any other part of the body. They're particularly important for demonstrating moods and relationships between people -lovers gaze, rivals stare, while phonies typically avoid eye contact. Pay more attention to look direction, eye shape, pupil size, length of gaze and what the eyebrows do.

VOICE: Words are not part of nonverbal communication, but the voice that speaks them is. Voice gives a wealth of info about standard background: culture, class, age, sex, birth place, color, race. Some research studies even suggest that you can tell an individual's height from their voice. Variations in volume, pitch and rhythm also demonstrate how we feel and whether something is important to us.

SMELL AND TASTE: Everyone has an individual odor and taste 'signature' that builds up in the mouth and in body hair. It can signify a person's general health, food choices and feelings of anger, fear or sexual arousal. Smell and taste are also crucial in creating a bond between people.

ENVIRONMENT: Nonverbal communication is about more than just what people do. It's also about the non-verbal declarations they make when they create their environment. Architecture, room size, furnishings style, light and temperature choices, personal privacy needs, in the home and at work, can all tell you what's important to someone, their standard personality and how they relate to others.

TOUCH: Touch, or absence of it, demonstrates how close people are and often indicates that strong feeling is being shared. Touch is also used in discussion to emphasize a point, and in power relationships to show control and dominance.

PHYSICAL FUNCTIONS: The body's physical functions, like breathing patterns, heart-rate, high blood pressure, skin color, sweat levels, skin temperature level and body fluids, show what somebody is feeling. They are instantaneous signals both of physical feeling and of psychological reaction.

INTERNAL BODY signs: The messages you give from inside are just as much a function of nonverbal communication as those it manifests on the outside. Know any internal photos or sounds that you experience when you come up with somebody or something. Know where any internal feeling is, and what it feels like-moving or still, heavy or light, warm or cold, relaxed or tense.

Decoding the message Once you've learned to observe closely and properly, then you can start to work out the meaning of what you're seeing. This isn't as simple as it might seem. As has been mentioned in the past, one single component of body language may not necessarily have just one particular meaning but several different ones, depending on the specific framework and situation.

First, think about a person's background when interpreting what they do.

Everyone's nonverbal communication has its roots in their culture and training: we learn the huge bulk of our nonverbal abilities when we are kids from the grownups around us. Naturally there are general signals that everybody uses, so most body language you see will fit the descriptions in this book (though these descriptions are based mainly on Western research and so won't always apply to people from simply African, Asian or Middle Eastern cultures).

Similarly, an individual's body language will always be personalized. Your best friend's inflamed blink may, for instance, be your associate's indication of uneasiness. So if you analyze your associate's body language as indicating the exact same as that of your friend, you'll spend a great deal of time wondering why she is irritated with you and trying needlessly to relax her down. Watch individuals' patterns over time to get what nonverbal professionals call 'standard behavior, which is their typical way of acting.

Also, when you observe a single aspect of nonverbal communication, have a look at completely what else is happening in the situation in which you see it What can you distinguish the person's whole body to get a complete picture of what is going on? What are their other body signals saying, do they confirm your interpretation or contradict it? How are other individuals reacting to what is going on do they see things in a different way from the way you do? What occurred right before and just after what you have seen that will help put it in framework and give it more meaning?

You should also look out for short set sequences of body language signals that always happen together, for example, when someone is surprised by an unanticipated sound, laughs to release the tension, then unwinds with a sigh. By having the ability to read not only the single hints-- the words of body language-- but also these sequences-or 'sentences'-- you'll be able to understand much more about what is going on.

When such a sequence has developed and become stylized in human social interaction- like the complex, nonverbal ritual we go through when we say goodbye to a person.

it often has a much different meaning from a spontaneous series so be prepared to analyze it differently.

You'll also, with practice, have the ability to identify broad patterns in an individual's nonverbal communication, where some components integrate to tell you something more general than just how they are feeling at this precise moment. Clusters of signals in the way somebody stands, looks and talks can show you what type of person they are or what their attitude to a specific aspect of life is.

Taking action Once you've observed and translated either your own or somebody else's nonverbal communication, then you can act.

You can use nonverbal communication to get more of what you want to achieve success in what you do, to create closer bonds with others, to help or support good friends or lovers and to improve your self-confidence.

When acting, you have 3 options Surprisingly, the first and usually the best choice is just to let your own body language instincts take control of. For everybody communicates nonverbally, all the time, as a natural, unconscious part of their lives.

If a friend is crying and you feel miserable for her, then you will immediately lean forward, and your eyes will spontaneously gain a gleam of wetness that signifies your empathy. You don't really need purposely to choose to do this your body will naturally and successfully mirror your feelings. So, in many situations, trusting your impulses is the best alternative.

Your 2nd alternative in any circumstance is to talk. As already pointed out, speaking is at times the best way to check out an issue, share experiences or offer convenience. Recall, however, that when you speak, you'll also be interacting nonverbally. This book will not only help you tell when words are most appropriate, but guide you towards using truly efficient body language to underline and support those words.

Your last alternative enters play when you choose to use some element of body language deliberately, or to intentionally change what you would naturally do. It may be that you feel considerate to a good friend, but don't know the best non-verbal way to show that. Or it could be that your natural expressions of sympathy aren't working and you need more options. If so, this book will help by detailing what develops success in non verbal communication, and by suggesting ways you can accomplish that success for yourself.

The real work is, of course, up to you. You need to collect info about body language, to start translating that information, to practice until you can use body language easily and it has the influence you really want. Even if you attain all this, body language might not be the answer to all your problems-but it will help you take advantage of what you think, what you feel, what you do, and-perhaps most crucial of all-who you are.

From the very first real moment you engage with another person, your shared body language is in continuous communication. You are telling them about yourself by the way you look, the way you move, the expression on your face and the tone of your voice - and if this sounds just too revealing, then assure yourself with the simple fact that they are telling you all about themselves in the same way.

This area of the book looks at how the process discussed above happens through social body language: how you can analyze properly what others are interacting to you, and how you in turn can be most reliable in what you communicate to them. It takes you through the steps from the preliminary meeting to holding a discussion, from comprehending a person - moment to moment, to analyzing their character over time. It explores how to make and keep friends, how to protect your time alone and how to appreciate that of other people-and finally how to make it through when you move from one to-one contact into the world at large.

Good to meet you

When you first meet a person, you have just 10 seconds to make an impression on them. Orto put it another way, in the first ten seconds after meeting a beginner, you will be making a particular impression on them whether you like it or not. Before you even open your mouth to speak, you non-verbally imprint the other person with your persona-- the image you present to the world-coming right across as reliable or inefficient, positive or nervous, friendly or standoffish. Even with a person you have met before, you can identify the whole tone of your contact by what your body language communicates at the very start.

Let's start, then, with the fundamentals. How do you initially make contact? The most essential way humans usually do so is with their eyes, so use yours efficiently. Do not use an off putting look but do keep your eyes on the person you're about to welcome so that, when they turn to you, you are ready to meet their look. If you open your eyes just slightly more commonly than typical, this approximates the short lived 'eyebrow flash that humans give spontaneously when they acknowledge another person, and which will instantly make your companion feel invited and appreciated.

After the preliminary welcoming, follow through that eye contact. Humans naturally turn toward those that they respect and value, so let your body and head direction concentrate on the other person, and battle any temptation to look or move away. Turning away signals. 'I fidget ...,' I feel inferior to you ... You'll be far more impressive if you deal with directly, lean in partially and show confidence and friendliness with a smile. (A great technique to remember if you are feeling worried and finding the encounter difficult is to smile rapidly and commonly three or four times, rather than try to maintain a repaired smile, which will die away gradually and embarrassingly).

Then you will be prepared to move into an official greetings routine involving words and touch. The direction in which your body is turned and angled toward the other person can instantly extend itself into offering your hand to be shaken. Do not be shy of this; humans are programmed to feel closer to someone they have touched, so losing out that part of the ritual means you lose the chance to produce a bond. A pointer from politicians, by the way, is to forget worrying about what to say, and just repeat the person's name as you look and touch. This not only makes your companion feel important but connects the person's name and face in your mind, making recall easier.

Throughout that, naturally, you won't be acting in a vacuum. The other person will be giving you clear signals regarding whether they authorize of what you are doing. Keep inspecting continuously to see how friendly or official they want to be, and after that adjust those five separate aspects of your greeting: eye contact, body lean, smile, touch and words. If meeting an opponent in an important sports match, for instance, you may want to tone down the smile and shake hands crisply and quickly. However, if your sister's new fiancé seems to think he needs to kiss you on both cheeks and you want to make him feel at ease, move closer in reaction to his extended forward lean, and determine from his movement just the correct time to offer initially one cheek, then the other.

However long you have understood an individual and whatever the framework of your relationship, there'll be a short stage of 'settling in after the initial greetings are over. Outwardly, you might appear just to be exchanging fundamental information about yourselves, in fact, on a non-verbal level there will be a lot more going on as you align your individual nonverbal communication styles to adapt to that complementary nonverbal communication rhythm called "rapport.

Accomplishing rapport is an instinctive human skill Babies do it even before birth, when their heart beats and body functions have a rhythm that matches those of their mother. By several months old, they will already have learned the other main component of rapport, turn-taking'- Child gurgles and smiles, Mom reacts with a coo and a smile, Child gurgles and smiles again.

As grownups, we no longer resort to gurgling to get a response! We do, however, use non-verbal cues to both 'match' and 'tumn-take." You match when both of you take up the exact same body posture, automatically copy gestures or emphatically nod just when your companion is absolutely saying a particular phrase. You turn-take naturally. alternating remarks movements and smiles. When your rapport is actually good, the words aren't important-your complementary body language says all of it

But what if things aren't working out? Individuals' bodies transfer to really different rhythms and there can be a mismatch. The symptoms are obvious and awkward. You feel ill at ease without understanding why. Then one of you gets itchy to speak while the other will not turn over the chance to talk. Rather than seamless turn-taking, you butt in and trip over one another or the silences get longer.

At this point, you may think it's because you have absolutely nothing in common. Your discomfort, however, is far more very likely to be due to a mismatch not of interests but of body language (specifically if your acquaintance is new and you have not yet learned whether you're compatible). Rather simply, your rhythms don't fit.

If you want to act to feel more comfortable with another person, use this body language technique: rather simply match their rhythms actively instead of leaving it to chance Observe the other person's posture, then move easily into copying it. I they change posture, do so also. Notice their rhythm of words and gestures, and follow it-a small nod when they nod, a slight lean forward when they say something absolutely, a flicker of a finger to mark their gestural rhythm. Be so tuned in to your companion that you turn-take naturally, speaking when they stop, decreasing when they want to begin.

For the first few minutes, intentionally matching an alien rhythm will feel uncomfortable: if it didn't, your body would already have done it automatically. And you have to be subtle about what you are doing or the other person might feel mocked or simulated. The secret is to keep your motions small and your paralleling shifts of posture or expression barely noticeable.

Keep going, however, and 2 things will eventually begin to happen. First, with practice, your body will feel more at ease and comfortable 2nd, as the other person is assured by the way you are integrating your responses with theirs, they will begin to integrate more with you, following your natural rhythm, moving into your natural position, smiling when you smile. Your 2 rhythms will coincide: you will build good relationships.

The art of discussions

It may be a cliché, but it is nonetheless true that the key to successful conversation is good listening--
this is what makes other people enjoy talking to you. But good listening isn't only about asking
appropriate questions.

The continuous non-verbal signals of your interest are actually more vital than your periodic verbal
questions, though well phrased.

The best way to send out the right signals is, of course, genuinely to listen, blocking out your own
thoughts and concentrating on what your companion is telling you. If you do this, you'll spontaneously
offer the body language that a very good listener does: you will look at your companion, you will
naturally lean towards them and angle your head partially to one side to hear them better. You will not
fidget or fiddle: your body will remain still and attentive, except for any slight matching of posture or
gesture.

For extra impact, you can also raise the volume on your nonverbal communication signs of attentiveness
Humans are naturally programmed to feel good when they get a response from another person, so the
more feedback you give to someone who is talking, the more valued they'll feel.

Begin by angling your body toward the person who's talking, and you will be offering a nonverbal invite
to speak.

Follow up by the regular head nod, which in human entities shows understanding. Make certain you nod
plainly and in synchrony with what your companion is saying, demonstrating your comprehension just
when they're highlighting an essential word or phrase. If they make a truly important point, give a long,
slow nod, which says, 'I'm taking you seriously' Beware, though, of the 'nodding dog syndrome";
unimportant nods signal that your mind is wandering, double nods tell others to accelerate their rate of
talking, while triple nods might bring people to a baffled standstill!

Also make sure to show your companion's emotions. When somebody speaks, what they want is for
others to laugh or cry together with them. 50 if your companion chuckles, make sure you at least smile,
if their body language shows sadness, let your expression become serious; if they snap as they recount a
story, mirror that inflammation by making your head nods faster and sharper.

And if you ask a question, add a minor tilt of the head, a small frown or a half-smile. This says 'I want to
really know more, not since you have been unclear, but because you have been so fascinating.' This
indication helps you query what someone is saying without threatening them, to motivate them to
clarify further. There is only one downside: your companion might believe you're so fascinated that they
carry on talking for hours!

THE SMOOTH TALKER

Have you ever listened to a digital voice, stripped of all visual and tonal signals, and become confused
and inflamed? If so, you will know that it's nonverbal communication that gives speech meaning, adding
important additional info about what's being said, creating mood and giving focus.

The first rule when speaking is to keep nonverbal contact with your listener. This contact can be forgotten as you focus only on the words. For instance, it's natural to avert regularly when you speak, to help the thinking process (see page 45): so it can be appealing to lose eye contact completely. If you catch yourself doing this intentionally glance at your listener whenever you can, to consist of and include them.

In addition, ensure that your body language shows what you are actually saying. The most fascinating speakers tend to use gestures, voice tone and facial expression to clarify and highlight their speech. So be aware of the words and expressions you use that are necessary to you so that you can provide the necessary emphasis. There are points of emphasis in every sentence, from 'Can you get me a new hair shampoo?' To when they say, 'Not that way, this way!' Each time, they nonverbally stress these points in specific.

Instinctive ways of doing this consist of: raising or reducing your tone, slowing down your speech, expanding your eyes, vanquishing the focus with a nod of your head or a wave of your hand called a 'baton gesture since it appears you are performing your own individual verbal orchestra). Naturally, if you're not used to differing your nonverbal communication like this to create interest, you might at first overdo it, and feel ridiculous or ashamed. So first watch how others have success, then experiment gradually with gestures or voice tones that come naturally.

To accomplish this, keep in mind the words that are very important to you, the ones you immediately worry then overemphasize that singing stress a little, with tone, pitch or speed. Add in movement -a head nod, then a really little forward lean that takes the head nod one stage farther. Use the baton gesture, letting your leading' hand (generally the right one) mark your head nod with the sort of movement that is most spontaneous for you. One great way to rehearse all this is on the phone: that way, there'll be no startled glances when you wave your arms around!

Finally, show real feeling in your speech. Know anything you say that has an emotional undercurrent. Allow yourself to experience some of that emotion: the embarrassment you felt when you dropped the spaghetti, the shock you felt when the waiter spilled the soup. Then let your body show your feeling naturally allow your voice to reflect it somewhat in tone and pitch, and your face to mirror it subtly in expression, particularly through your eyes, eyebrows and mouth, the main channels for emotional communication. You'll draw your listener into your experience, making it much more brilliant for them.

STABILIZING ACT

Much of the art of discussions depends on creating a balance between everyone's contribution-an extension of the turn-taking rhythm of rapport described earlier. Effective speakers manage this balance by utilizing non-verbal signals to show they've completed speaking, or that they want to contribute. Sadly, not everybody knows these signals, uses them or react to them.

If you're the listener, it works to know that when a speaker pauses for longer than usual or decreases their speech, they're probably prepared for you to talk. They may accompany this with a shift in voice pitch, direct eye contact and a little Thand-over gesture that waves you in to take your turn. The secret, for you as a listener, is not even to attempt to talk unless you see these things happening, or you are going to find yourself interrupting. If, when the signals do happen, you actually do not want to contribute, then and the verbal technique of asking another question to urge the speaker on, you can decrease your turn by keeping eye contact and nodding slowly, or by using the 'query expression mentioned previously.

If you are the speaker, make the above signals obvious when you want to hand over. Equally do not give such signals if you want to keep talking if somebody disrupts you, it's often not since they're disrespectful, but as you have given some unclear non verbal check in the middle of a sentence. If you want to hold on to your turn, keep away from eye contact, do not stop briefly, raise your voice slightly and prevent yourself from making any turn-giving gestures.

The worst conversational problem is not getting to deviate at all. If you're stuck with the party bore mentioned earlier, start by giving him (or her) the natural signals we make in conversation when we want to speak. Get eye contact and, at the slightest pause, inhale audibly as if you're preparing to say something and give a short cough to accentuate you. Increase your rate of nodding to give the message 'Rush and finish.'

If all this stops working, be antisocial! Hard-heartedly stop giving the typical good-listener signs. Lose eye contact, stop nodding, blank your expression to give no emotional feedback. Look to one side as though sidetracked. Raise a finger or hand-- a sign we learn in school that still, for adults, means, 'I want to talk." If, after all that your companion still continues, she or he isn't worth listening to disrupt mercilessly until you get some attention, and use that chance to proceed!

It goes without saying that if you yourself get any of these I'm bored body language signals when you're talking, there's only one correct reaction a polite and immediate hand-over, and an inner resolution to shut up and listen for a while.

Mind magic

Whenever you engage with somebody, you naturally learn more about them and the way they think. Current nonverbal communication discoveries Suggest that with a keen eye and ear you can understand what people are thinking and how their minds work in really particular ways. According to psychologists, our body language gives clues to how our brains are working. Quite just, what we think of inside our heads we reveal externally with our bodies.

As you probably know from your own experience, the people and experiences that we experience in the world around all of us have some inner association in our heads perhaps in the form of a picture, a sound or perhaps an odor, taste or touch. If you doubt that you do this, remember what color the sheets are on your bed at the moment, or imagine what your favorite track would seem like dipped into half speed.) Everything we store in our brains has a representation there-- even if we aren't able to see a completely vibrant picture of it or hear a totally clear noise.

So, to analyze the body language clues to what is going on in someone's head, start with the most basic reduction: how is an individual using their thought processes? 2 American psychologists, Richard Bandler and John Grinder, have suggested that an individual's eye motions show which notice they're thinking about-in other words, whether they're remembering or thinking of something seen, heard, touched, smelled or tasted.

Bandier and Grinder suggest that if what an individual is thinking of is something they have seen, they'll search for or defocus, sit straight up, raise their eyebrows, furrow their eyebrow horizontally and breathe quicker. If they're thinking of a noise, they'll look to the side, tilt their heads as if listening and breathe evenly, if what a person is thinking about is some feeling), they'll look down and to the right, lean forward, round their shoulders, breathe deeply.

More particularly, if an individual is recalling something that they actually saw or heard, their eyes will also slightly move to their left-but if they're thinking of seeing or hearing something that has not actually occurred yet their eyes will move to their right. If they're thinking in words (what you may call speaking with themselves"), then they will look down and to their left, and typically make tiny motions of throat or lips

Each of these eye motions takes less than a split second: you may not even register them. They'll be strung together in series of some lots, and so you can't perhaps track every idea as it happens. But you can certainly get a good deal of info about whether someone usually thinks in photos, words or emotions, and whether a particular memory or creative thought is being experienced through any one specific sensory channel. Sometimes, with a clear signal, you can tell whether somebody is remembering what they've seen, and ask, "What did they appear like?' before they have now informed you about their thoughts.

MIND MOVEMENTS

Having got a broad idea of what somebody is considering through their eye motions, you can then start being more particular by also watching their head and limbs perform what are called 'mime movements Try asking someone how many glasses of red wine they had last night. They will see in their mind's eye by looking partially upwards their eyes might also repair from left to right, with a small look to mark each item they're remembering. The rest of their body will include additional info: their head may give a tiny nod for each fix; they might tap out, with a finger, hand or foot, the exact number that they remember. With careful observation and precise analysis, you will not only be able to tell what they're going to say, but also, if what they say doesn't fit with what you saw, you can challenge the mistake.

Head and limb movements, in specific, give an exceptional amount of information about how we 'see things in our heads. So, for example, the shape an individual traces with their hands and head will be representative of a shape they're picturing in their minds. The relative size of what they draw will be telling you the relative value of things to them. The speed at which they make movements will show you how much excitement, stress or satisfaction they feel about what is in their mind. The position of their gestures in the air might well show whether what they're thinking of happened in the past (gesture to the left or behind), present (gesture directly in front) or future (gestures to the right or far in front). And if their movement equates a real action, that may well show that they have done that action or are meaning to do it.

Try this test: without clarifying why, ask a friend to describe her job. Watch the movements she uses. She might trace several stabbing motions with her hands while at the exact same time shaking her head dramatically from side to side. Her movements might start high in the air when she talks about her boss and gradually come down as she describes her colleagues. Her gestures might speed up as she explains about just what her latest task includes, moving from the left as she describes beginning it until ultimately, as she envisions completing it, she makes a big, chopping movement over to her right. Even with no words at all, you will be able to rate her real compatibility with her job-just as you would if she gave a completely different image by utilizing gentle, flowing gestures to trace a circle in the air before finally lifting her hands in a harmonious and relaxed way.

Psychological expressions Finally, as you watch eye movements and check gestures, observe a person's facial expression, for that will show you just how they feel about what they're saying. The sequences are simple to read, though they can be tiny, short lived and exceptionally variable. Some of the more common expressions are: a minor smile and a widening of the eyes just as if to see more,' demonstrating that an individual feels good; a small frown, a down-drooping of the mouth and a constricting of the eyes to 'see less." indicating disapproval; a sideways movement of the mouth and a screwing-up of the eyes, demonstrating that they're wary or uncertain.

With practice, particularly with somebody you know well you can be extremely accurate at 'mind reading.' So if, when asked which club she went to last night, your good friend initially looks up and to the left, then sideways and left, then down, she's probably envisioning what the club looked a lot like, what the music was like and what experiences she experienced. Put all that together with her blank expression when she looks up; a curl of the lip, a headshake and a pushing-away gesture when she wants to the side, and a small smile and self-touching movement when she looks down. If you know your friend adequately well to put meaningful flesh on the bones of her nonverbal communication, you might be not too away if you thought that the decor was neutral and the music was awful-- but there was someone there she felt good about.

Reading personalities Using nonverbal communication to analyze somebody's personality isn't something new. As far back as the Middle Ages, people thought that physical appearance had a one-to-one connection with character. A huge nose in a man, for example, meant that he had a huge sexual hunger, for reasons that are fairly obvious; a small head meant that someone was unintelligent. This medieval nonverbal communication was fairly soon discredited-our body parts simply do not indicate what we are like as people.

More just recently, psychologists have been rethinking. For while the components we inherit, such as a big nose or a little head, bear no relation to what sort of person we're inside, the components of our body language that we develop throughout a lifetime. If, for example, a person is an easy-going person and really relaxed, her body posture will be loose and fluid since this is how her muscles are. Conversely, if she is really anxious and tightens her muscles a good deal of the time, then she might end up with tense, raised shoulders.

If you want to evaluate people's character, do not look at their individual gestures or short lived expressions. Look instead at their more long-term, consistent, lifelong nonverbal communication patterns -typical posture, typical gestures, normal series of eye movement, expression and touch. With this checklist in mind, observe a person gradually and you'll be able to draw conclusions about what their patterns mean.

To begin you off, this area covers three frequently recognized character structures, and goes on to define the body language that usually chooses them.

One aspect hidden everyone's personality is which of the senses they prefer. Does a person revel most in what they see, hear or touch? (The senses of odor and taste are normally peripheral, crucial only in circumstances like eating or love making.) Most human beings do have a small choice for one of these, but some people have a very unique taste for one sense or the other, which informs their personality and can often show through noticeably in their nonverbal communication.

Lookers tend to have good posture but tense shoulders. They're typically thin, with tight lips. Certainly they are going to choose outfits and furniture for visual impact-- they feel good inside when they see attractive things. Not only this, but they also think generally in images, which causes horizontal brow-furrowing, so they may have forehead wrinkles on an otherwise unlined face.

Listeners think noise is important; and words are also important. Their normal posture is with head partially down and to one side, as if listening, or with one hand up to their face or ear - the telephone posture.' When thinking something through, you will often see their lips move, as if speaking to themselves. They really love rhythm, and may beat out mental riffs on tables, on chair arms or in the air. They'll have the automobile stereo set to switch on when they start the ignition.

Touchers-- who are usually really psychological people-are typically rounded fit. They may not actually be plump, but they tend to lean in, and have somewhat rounded shoulders and full lips. They breathe deeply, relocation in a rather loose, relaxed way and typically have deep voices. Their style is based on how things feel instead of look, so they will choose for convenience and softness rather than style.

There are pros and cons to each sensory choice. Tending toward one rather than another doesn't put an individual at a downside in life, though it may mean that they're more suited to some tasks than others. Never ever, for instance, ask a listener to tell you what to wear to a party, while fashion guidance from a looker will ensure that you look superb-but won't ensure that you feel comfortable. Similarly, if you identify that your interior designer is a toucher, you might want to hire somebody else -though you may also consider having a sensual affair with him or her.

Check to see if you yourself have a strong choice for one sense. If you have prepared for prospective issues when you meet someone with a strong choice for another. If you're a looker and a good friend is a listener, drawing him a picture of your new apartment will be worthless; tell him about it instead. If he, in return, tries to define his new girlfriend, you might really need him to show you a picture before you can actually be passionate about the relationship.

A lot more subtly lookers, listeners and touchers vary in their standard communication styles. A looker will actually really need to look a lot while talking-which may make a listener feel gotten into, on the other hand, a listener, who tends to avert while speaking, may make a looker feel unappreciated. And if, during a squabble, your toucher good friend moves closer to get peace of mind, he isn't attacking your space, just following his sensory preferences, if you embrace him, he will find it easier to feel good again.

Another well-established character distinction is that between extrovert and introvert-people who consistently like to be sociable as compared to people who to, they'll make 'escape motions with their feet or hands, as if trying to get away.

Not surprisingly, extroverts act really differently. They will spontaneously turn towards people, lean forward and keep eye contact for long periods of time. They talk more energetically than introverts do, to encourage other people's reactions and the stimulus that provides. Their gestures and expressions seem more joyful when they're with you just as they feel fired up and comfortable when around others. They touch more, and react to touch, perhaps by cuddling up in an effort to get yet more sensation

Each character type should be treated differently. Draw an introvert off into a quieter area, or one where you can be alone. Do not attack her space, either by moving closer or by demanding too much eye contact, talk quietly and use touch with care. Just remember that it's not that she does not like you-it's that your presence may be too much for her to handle. An extrovert, on the other hand, can take all the stimulus you can give. Move closer, talk quicker, give eye contact and touch her.

Be prepared, too, for extremely deviant relationships with each character type. You alone may not be enough for the extrovert, who will typically like to be out and about, socializing with others, in loud, promoting environments. The introvert will be at her happiest in intimate situations, with dim lights, soft music and one-to one contact

OK AND NOT OK A third character difference is that between the 'OK' person and the 'Not OK' person. Eric Berne, the founder of the mental school of Transactional Analysis (TA), which specifies our technique to life in regards to the roles we use in our deals with others, coined these terms to describe 2 basic personality types-people who are generally content with themselves, and people who feel inferior and insecure.

An OKAY person's standard posture is upright, with shoulders firm and square, head raised and body evenly and easily well balanced. She moves briskly and without hesitation, and her expression is vibrant with an irreversible half-smile. If you get near to her, you may see tiny lines at the corners of her mouth that slope upward an indication that she smiles more than she sulks.

A Not OKAY person's posture is fractionally stooped, her back partially bent: she might look dropped as she walks or sits, with head down towards her chest. Her movements are sluggish, tired and forced, and her expression exhausted and sad. Her mouth corner lines slope partially downward, which is an indication that she sulks more than she smiles

If you meet a Not OK person you will be instantly wary. You may feel, without knowing why, that though they are rather lively at this specific party in the long term they will not be much fun to be with. Such feelings are instinctive and should be observed. Humans have an integrated defense mechanism that-unless overruled by duty or compassion towards another person alerts them to the non-verbal signs of someone who suffers long-term distress, and cautions them to avoid.

People with Not OKAY body language are at a social disadvantage, finding it tough to make contact and maintain relationships. And, because body language ends up being more fixed with time, such people might find themselves becoming more and more isolated. Be cautioned! Just look in the mirror and be truthful with yourself, what does your body language say about you? Is it sliding towards the OK or the Not OKAY?

if you are the latter, take steps now. For an instant influence, try adopting the OKAY nonverbal communication that you do not have. Sit more upright, move quicker, smile more and take upward' as your nonverbal communication direction. This will not only indicate more positive things to other individuals, but will also actually make you temporarily feel better about yourself. The maxim 'Put on a happy face actually does work

For much deeper, longer-term change, however, you'll need to do more than just act differently on the surface area. If you actually want to modify your personal body language on the outside, you will actually need to move your mindsets on the inside. If you build your self-confidence through organizing your life, then your body language will eventually shift. You'll clean your facial expression will raise, you're going to look more cheerful and the change will be real and permanent.

You're at a party, a conference or maybe a night class. You are stalling, looking straight ahead, with no expression on your face, clutching your beverage. You are imitating this as you fidget of being turned down if you approach someone, or as you feel that being seen to try to find company signifies social failure. Although company is what you actually want, what you are signifying is just the opposite Your message is, 'I do not want to be approached. I am not interested.

Individuals who are successful in group gatherings have the ability to integrate non-verbal 'activity with non-verbal 'approachability. This doesn't mean that they are extroverts (who choose a great deal of social stimulation, but aren't necessarily socially active in gaining it). Popular people have a method of body language, gesture, expression and eye focus that keeps them continuously and energetically seeking contact with others

Begin to practice these strategies the minute you get in a brand-new place. Mosey but purposefully from place to place, 'sweeping the room' to catch people's eyes. Keep moving, you aren't, at this point, going to stop and speak to anybody. Your eye contact is a non-verbal signal to show you're socially readily available, as well as enabling you to spot other people who feel the exact same. Keep your expression friendly rather than flirty (see page 61), with a half-smile and open gestures. And relax! A positive and friendly person is an attractive figure to others who aren't rather so self-assured

When you reach an individual, make certain it's with somebody who, by previously catching your eye, has already signified their approachability. One of the reasons we may struggle socially is that we judge whom to approach by whether they look interesting in general instead of whether they look thinking about us in particular. Then we feel turned down if they don't respond favorably to a contact, which, in reality they've not invited

If the person you're approaching is a man, it's best to advance from the side, and if lady, approach from the front, as these directions are most reassuring to each gender. Research undertaken in 1974 suggests that, as men are typically more likely to be challenged face to deal with, and women most likely to be assaulted from behind, our bodies naturally, though for a moment, press the panic button when approached from these directions, even with friendly intent.

The socially accepted routine is to approach adequately close that a person registers your presence. Then stop briefly for consent to enter their space, which they'll give with continuing eye contact, a comforting half-smile or an unconscious beckoning gesture. You may give a minute head nod (in apes, this is a gesture of reassurance), and after that an answering smile, a relocation closer and a greeting. You do not really need to make excuses for why you've come over. If that person is also by themselves, they are going to be relieved you've approached them.

If the person you approach is actually accompanied, but their good friend has temporarily wandered off to another room, the bar or the bathroom, then offer reassuring signals when the friend returns. Your nonverbal communication needs to say. I'm not taking your husband ... I'm not annexing your sweetheart ...' You can accomplish this by literally making space for the newbie, significantly opening the set you form part of two enable the other person in, turning towards them, making certain that you give them eye contact, and smiling at them for the first not many minutes of the interaction. As they start to feel assured and begin to relax you are going to find that you all naturally shift position to form an equivalent triangle, calming down to getting rapport.

Chapter 10: Going with the Crowd

What if you are making contact with more than someone? Signing up with a group can be a very real difficulty. There is always a period of 'initiation, a time of waiting to be seen as 'OK' before people will actually accept you; this has its roots in ape conduct where newbies need to be completely checked out initially in case they are a danger to the colony.

So choose your group with care, judging from the non-verbal signals which one it is best to technique if loud voices and a lot of activity tell you that group members already know each other, they will not quickly make you invite, while groups where only one person is holding forth will make it tough for you to make your mark. Choose instead for a group that is small enough for everybody to participate, big enough for individuals to turn and talk with one another, or one in which you know a person you can use as your passport in.

It's hardly ever acceptable for anyone to start contributing as quickly as they join the group. The exceptions are high-status people such as party hosts or VIPs, extrovert and dominant people who might unthinkingly try to take over when they join a group, and children-who are forgiven as they have not yet learned the social rules. For everybody else, the unwritten law is that you spend a sensible time giving non-verbal signals to show you're safe staying quiet, watching whoever is speaking, gradually presuming a rapportful rhythm with everyone else so that you laugh when they laugh and nod when they nod.

You can, however, reduce your acceptability period by exaggerating these signals just slightly so that they are more visible and so that people automatically see you as safe earlier. So, when you are finally given an actual chance to speak, follow these standards. You'll generally get your reverse again quickly and your position in the group will then be established.

WHO'S YOUR BEST FRIEND? When you meet a person briefly, your aim is to assure them, your body language signals security, approval and rapport. But when you both begin to build a friendship, the communication procedure then shifts from short term reassurance to longer term bonding. Nonverbally, your aim becomes to learn as much as you can about each other, to be as comparable as you can be

Here, body language techniques as such are reasonably meaningless. The procedure of forming a deep bond with someone is so complex and lengthy that it can happen only on a subconscious level: if you try to rush it on with mindful and purposeful actions, your conduct will appear incorrect. Where body language comes in useful though, is in monitoring how the process is progressing, and in building the best environment for friendship

When you are on track, you're going to find that both of you are opening your sensory channels spontaneously-as if to get info from one another-with broader eyes, longer gazes and "punctured' ears that can take in more. You'll be giving each other more information, too, by sitting visibly closer together, facing one another more directly, making your faces more meaningful, touching more regularly and talking more loudly and with greater emphasis

This isn't the exact same kind of physical nearness you get with a love partner, but you will develop increasingly comparable nonverbal communication series that parallel your significantly similar ideas and emotions. You can help this process by setting up the right non verbal environment for development: arranging to go to events together so that you share experiences, and rotating these with more intimate encounters where you can talk deeply, with lots of eye contact and physical closeness

Given these environments, in time you are going to progressively 'match' (see page 22), either straight matching postures, gestures or movements, or mirroring' by copying with the opposite hand or foot. You'll also parallel your friend not so much with the obvious signs of rapport, but by recreating subtler series like anxious habits and vocal accents.

You might start wearing the exact same style of clothes, listening to the same sort of music, eating at the same kind of restaurant. This isn't just a case of like brings in like. By adopting the same style as each other, you're intentionally telling the world that you are the exact same sort of person. Anthropologists call these 'tie signs.' They're most obvious in teenage years, where everybody in the exact same group will go around wearing the exact same badge or tee-shirt. But grownups display tie signs, too-just come up with Gucci purses and gym memberships!

As your friendship develops, you 'd expect all this proof of bonding to grow, which it does for a while. But interestingly, it fades with time as you be progressively comfortable and familiar with each other. So if you're with a good friend you've known for years. perhaps since youth, you typically do not give each other obvious attention. You may sit separately, side by side, not touching, not holding eye contact. Your voices are low, almost unstimulated, your postures relaxed and unexcited. You may not obviously match gestures or styles. It can seem as if you're not interested.

What has happened, quite just. is that the learning stage is over. You know how the other person relocations, 50 you do not really need to face them directly to see it. You notice that you're close, so you do not really need blindingly apparent matching or mirroring to prove it. All the proof of resemblance has ended up being very discreetly integrated. Your breathing will be in perfect synchrony, your blinks will match to a fraction of a second and, if one of you turns white with uneasiness or pink with shame, the other will fade or color up slightly, too. When walking along you will not need to indicate that you want to turn right and cross the roadway, as you would with an acquaintance. With an old good friend, the turn will be made and the road crossed without either of you recognizing that micro-clues took care of every little thing

What if you are trying to make friends not with a sole individual but with a group; an existing, established circle of friends. There are more insecurities and hostilities-- even if you are introduced as someone's partner, people will stress in case you're a hazard. Will you be more attractive or intelligent than existing members? Will you interfere with the group dynamic?

As in any relationship, talking will help. A few extended discussions with individuals will develop a bond as you switch experiences and feelings. However, don't expect to talk in the group itself for rather a little bit of time. Developed inner circles often efficiently gag new members until they are sure of them, by not offering them any turn taking signs. Attempting to defeat this procedure by butting in or speaking over people can cause quite a frightening closing of ranks, as you're ignored, 'talked over' or greeted with a courteous but stony silence.

Make development, instead, with your non-verbal behavior. Make sure that your body language is always unthreatening to individual members and non-challenging to the existing dynamic. Tend not to go first or try to take the lead; hang back for meals, drinks or anything where an informal line-up might form. Understand unmentioned territory' laws in the group-- don't, for example, take a seat before examining whether you have chosen somebody's special chair. Keep in mind any group customs, like always watching a specific television program, and don't challenge these. Offer to assist with low-status jobs like cleaning dishes rather than expecting to do the high-status ones.

The first signs that you're being accepted will be non-verbal. You'll be paid more attention in the group, looked and smiled at more and offered turn-taking signals so that you get to speak. When you do speak, you can then evaluate your success by the quality of the silence; is it still courteous, with somewhat avoided inattentive eyes and slight fidgets, or is it relaxed, with head-on-one-side listening and nods of agreement? Notice if you are being offered more closeness and touch, in the form of spontaneous pats and pushes, or an increased willingness to 'squash up' next to you. As time passes, expect to get not only your own literal territory, like a place at the table, but also your own metaphorical territory for example, a subject on which you're considered an expert. In the end, body language within the group will develop an empathy of the sort you 'd find in a one-to-one friendship, with unconscious matching, a natural awareness of individuals' state of minds and a mutual ability to anticipate what everyone is going to do next just through nonverbal communication.

WHEN FRIENDSHIPS END

Whether they're one-to one or group alliances, tons of friendships fade in time. Furious arguments may produce unmendable rifts, but more frequently, people just lose their common interests and drift apart. You know what you feel about your friends but, given the social convention of not being in advance about such things. how can you tell what they feel about you?

The easy way to check this is to examine all the non-verbal signals. If you're trying to evaluate a group circumstance, then check the signs between you and each group member.) If you make a small approach a good friend, they reciprocate-an unwilling good friend shies away. If you offer eye contact to an old good friend, that's accepted-a retreating good friend blinks or can't meet your look. A buddy will match you, even if in extremely subtle ways-a bad friend will inequality, so that you run into one another, go out of step. pass dishes awkwardly at table.

Look, too, at whether your nonverbal communication still indicates equality. Are you turn-taking in conversation, or is one of you now doing all the talking and the other doing all the listening? is one of you still expressing feeling, while the other presents a blank face?

Similarly, as a relationship dies, you can typically spot negative emotions. If a friend fidgets or fiddles, making what are called 'get away movements with hands or feet throughout your time together, then you should beware. If she or he reacts to your need for assistance with a vigorous voice tone, or stops working to hide a smile when you are in an embarrassing situation, then the writing is on the wall.

Talking is the best possible way to resolve such problems a complete and frank conversation to settle things one way or another. But what if you feel nervous about speaking openly? What if you're incorrect and a friend is offended-or what if you're right and she's hostile? In this case, see what happens if you intentionally withdraw from the friendship much more rapidly than your good friend is doing-non-verbally. Next time you meet, be the one who loses eye contact, mismatches, holds back on emotional expression or sits far away. Let your natural ambivalence show through, indicating by body language that you are uncertain of the friendship

If you keep doing this one of 2 things will happen. Either your friend will, with a sigh of relief, think that you too have lost interest and will not contact you again Or she'll worry and ask you what's wrong. Either way you are going to have moved closer to a decision whether to end your friendship or to renew it again you're right and she's hostile? In this case, see what happens if you deliberately withdraw from the friendship a lot more rapidly than your good friend is doing-non-verbally. Next time you meet, be the one who loses eye contact, mismatches, holds back on psychological expression or sits far away. Let your natural uncertainty show through, suggesting by nonverbal communication that you are uncertain of the friendship

If you keep doing this one of two things will happen. Either your friend will, with a sigh of relief, think that you too have lost interest and will not call you again or she will worry.

Up to this point, we have explored only the body language of interaction. Actually, you don't always want company

It's well-known that humans need time to themselves every day. Fascinatingly enough nevertheless, we also need it on a second-by 2nd basis. Although much of our day is spent looking listening, talking or doing, every three seconds we need to 'slip away,' to give our brains time to process what is really happening to think of what we want to say next. The psychological name for this is 'downtime' (as opposed to 'uptime, when we're interacting with the world). A person in downtime may tilt her head away and shift her shoulders at an angle. Or she may look to the right or left for a fraction of a second. These are known in the trade as 'conjugate lateral eye motions. If she chews her lips or captures her breath, her mind is in processing mode.

You have now definitely already seen many people in downtime on thousands of different occasions, but you have probably not understood exactly what you were seeing or what that meant. Realizing that a person is actually in downtime enables you to respond in a proper style, to keep pace with their thinking and to stay away from clashes when, for instance, they're trying to recall something in downtime, and you are expecting them to engage with you in uptime.

So if somebody averts momentarily when you're speaking to them, don't assume they're not interested or effort to continue regardless. They're for a moment turned off from the outside world, and you are going to get much farther if you slow your speech, pause and provide space to think And if someone slips into downtime when they themselves are talking-typically this will happen at the very starting and very end of their contribution; it means they need to think before continuing Let them! Do not disrupt with an important question and do not confuse downtime signals with hand-over ones (see page 26), and just launch in with your own comments. Instead, wait until their head lifts and their gaze go back to yours before you communicate again

THE COLD SHOULDER

Just like we need short-lived downtime, all of us also need extended, solitary downtime. We really need it if we're concentrating if we've been psychologically overactive, when we're under strain or just really need to recuperate from day-to-day tensions.

Do not puzzle this need for alone time with introversion, which is a basic, deep-rooted level of sensitivity to stimulation. Those periods when we're desperate for solitude take place in specific contexts when, like sophisticated computer systems, we really need time to procedure and recuperate from the mass of stimuli being available in from the outside world.

If you do not get the alone time you really need, the internal signals will increase. You'll start to feel nervous, tense and irritated. These are signs that your body needs help just as definitely just as if it were hungry or thirsty. So, rather knowingly and clearly show your body language withdrawal. Put your head down or put your hands on each side of your eyes as blinkers' or over your ears as 'plugs.' Close your eyes if you can-- the ultimate of saying, nonverbally. "Go away. I don't want to be bothered."

Set up physical barriers to Produce a wall around yourself with obstructing arm, books, papers, a chaic or that most obvious of buffers, a closed door. Put your own individual 'markers' such as your coat or bag, on each side of you, so people know that they can't take a seat or technique. Stick your elbows out and let your entire body signal, 'Give me space.'

You could also use the natural hostility signals that your body uses intuitively to make you appear more aggressive towards people who demand attempting to engage when you do not want them to. You might find yourself frowning, getting tight lipped or raising your shoulders-the classic cold shoulder treatment. Sending out these signals indiscriminately isn't, obviously, a pretty good idea: you might appear from your hard-won downtime to find you no longer have any friends! But if you really do need to be left in peace for a while, then your body's natural way of protecting you might well work.

SORRY TO INTERRUPT

What if you're the one on the receiving end of this non-verbal avoidance? First, recognize that such conduct is not meant personally and that it is a genuine cry for assistance The best thing is to avoid, for doing so will, in the long run, allow you to maintain a much better relationship

If you just have to engage, check or ask something, someone who needs time alone will react better if you use an official 'alert signal beforehand. 50 if you're approaching from a short distance, stop while still between 12 and 4 feet 14 and 1.2 m) away, within the social range zone and before you go into the more intimate personal range zone. Knock on the door, if there is one between you, and clear your throat (a courteous signal of disturbance used even with mountain gorillas) instead of speaking immediately.

Once you have caught the attention of a person who needs alone time, keep your interaction to a minimum. Minimize rapport signals. If another person's body is already overstimulated, then your close method, your forward lean, your demand for eye contact will actually lead to their going through a panic reaction. Instead, stay back, keep standing to show that you're leaving quickly, and do not get rid of any protective barriers Speak gently, quietly and gradually so as not to overload their system with more stimulation and, as quickly as you have what you want, leave.

And be assured. The body never takes more alone time than it needs. So in all possibility, if you appreciate their needs, the person who's been non-verbally indicating you to disappear will soon start non-verbally indicating that they really want you to come back.

As quickly as you step outside your house, you will notice a shift in the sort of body language you use. Public nonverbal communication is discreetly different from private nonverbal communication, because you don't know the people involved, and you are going to most likely never have a real chance to be familiar with them. The result is that, surrounded by all these strangers, your nonverbal communication will usually become extremely safeguarded in public.

In public, you may well find yourself using a version of cold shoulder body language, acting as if other people aren't actually there. On a crowded train, for instance, you may handle a defocused look, studiously looking through a person although their face is just a couple of inches from yours: you may shrink your neck into your shoulders and psychologically 'deafen' yourself to the discussion of the couple next to you-and remain perfectly immobile as if absolutely uninformed that the person next to you has his left arm jammed up against your right ear.

TRAFFIC CONTROL You can't ignore others for ever though. So an entire set of non-verbal signals has evolved to cope with times when you have no choice but to be included. The most standard kind of interaction is having to move along a street in conjunction with others you walk in parallel you surpass and are surpassed you meet head-on. To succeed in these deals, remember that the worst method is walking, which non-verbally signals to others that you're likely to stop, and makes them disappointed and restless Instead, move quickly and actively. Give yourself Some room by 'enlarging your body. squaring your shoulders and sticking your elbows out. Focus your look sufficiently into the middle distance that anybody approaching thinks you won't see them, so intuitively moves out of the way. This technique will get you along quickly and easily as long as you can keep up the momentum.

If you hit a 'log jam' and get stuck, change methods instantly and twitch, making yourself as thin and as little as possible, squeezing past people carefully to stay away from body contact Notice, by the way, how men in a squeeze-past' situation turn towards someone just as if to face any possible attack, while women turn away, their arms right across bosoms and genital areas. Recall, too, that people have a natural propensity to 'signal' that they want to change direction by pointing their bodies in the direction they wish to go. Signals like this will be registered, typically automatically, by those behind you, who will then fall back to enable you to make your move.

ARE YOU BEING SERVED? Another common sort of public interaction is with people who serve you, in stores, restaurants and beauty salons, for instance. The first step to success is to engage. Be clear and powerful: you are typically competing with other consumers for attention, and a busy service worker often has other things on his/her mind. Shoot your hand up firmly and significantly as you wait the side of the roadway to call a taxi, advance and take a look around confidently for eye contact as you get in a dining establishment.

Expect some sort of recommendation. Look for a smile and head nod, so that you know you have been seen and that action is being taken. If an acknowledgment isn't forthcoming, then stress your signals instead of simply waiting Try a wave of the hand or a shift in your posture that captures the person's peripheral vision, or a gesture sufficiently from your body that it is truly visible.

The second phase in service interaction is shared rapport building. Here, the person who's serving you is working just as hard as you are to acquire contact through body language. Do not expect the exact same kind of intimacy' as you get with friends most service staff are trained not to take part in too much interaction and will feel uncomfortable if you move too close or keep too much eye contact.

Always use clear non-verbal signals. Because public spots are typically loud and words can be misunderstood, and also since you're just "passing through' and don't have a chance to build up a relationship, you need to clearly show what your needs are. So instead of simply saying which drink you really want at the bar, highlight your choice non-verbally by pointing. And in response to an inquiry, nod or shake your head to highlight the appropriate words and saying 'yes' or 'no'.

Take particular care in demonstrating when a transaction is complete or incomplete. If you want to show to a restaurant waiter that you're ready to order, for instance, do not keep the menu open, as this is a signal that you are still deciding. And if you want to ask an extra question of the sales assistant after she's covered your goods, use the 'query gesture of head on one side and a minor smile, or the turn-taking gesture of in-drawn breath and raised finger, or she's going to carry on to the next customer instantly.

Aim to leave service staff with a favorable memory of you so that they treat you favorably next time. The best way is to bid farewell using rapport; ful nonverbal communication of a smile and direct eye contact to show that you're not dehumanizing' them, as many people do. But be aware of the management's attitude, if your body language style makes a worker engage with you too completely, that might mean a reprimand for them later. Even the friendliest waiter will get edgy if you insist on prolonged attention when he has consumers waiting and the one in charge is watching.

WHO IS REALLY IN CHARGE? Perhaps one of the most stressful examples of public interaction is handling people in authority-a traffic officer walking by as you're feeding the meter, a ticket inspector boiling down the train. For though in theory they're there to serve you, they're also there to 'police the system. Their body language is carefully developed to signal superiority, their uniform includes 'height and width-enhancers' such as a helmet or peaked cap.

Their training shows them how to stare you down dominantly. Your body language reacts immediately and spontaneously to this, whether you're guilty of anything. Just watch the responses of reputable and innocent guests the next time that ticket inspector appears: necks tilt into a heads-down' defensive position, there is a flurry of anxious gestures to find the ticket. and some people will begin making 'leave motions of hands or feet.

So what is the best way of dealing with this kind of circumstance? Neither 'dominance body language to withstand authority nor submissive nonverbal communication to soothe it is the most efficient reaction: authority figures are trained to be suspicious of both and react accordingly. Rather, let your body language signal relaxed equality with just a touch of deference; that will give the needed message: 'I acknowledge and respect your role here.

If the police pull you over on the road, for example, enable your nonverbal communication to signify that you're not a danger. If it's appropriate, stay seated. If the officer asks you to get out of your vehicle, don't pull yourself up to your full height, but keep your shoulders slightly hunched and your head slanted slightly down. Look but do not look directly or make confrontational eye contact, when combined with other supremacy signals, gives a difficult message. And don't immediately move into a complete rapport building sequence, as this can be seen as an attempt to be over-friendly instead, tone every little thing down so that you keep an enjoyable expression.

Act quickly and helpfully. We're not talking here about snapping to attention; but if needed to produce your driving license, do so willingly and without delay, and if asked questions, address them in a peaceful tone and without doubt. You may well be feeling unstable, for your body will, as pointed out in the past, automatically move into 'panic' mode; so try to keep one's cool, breathing deeply and steadily

Finally, expect the moment when the officer psychologically signs you off. For there's a point in each interaction when, having given clear signals of supremacy to prevent any issues from developing an authority figure relaxes just partially as they judge you're not a threat. Once this happens, then you can begin to react in a more friendly way to their less regulated gestures, their more relaxed posture or their growing smile. Understand, though, that if you take this too far, they may feel threatened again; if they return to their authority body language, you should instantly revert to your previous recommendation' behavior.

IN WITH THE CROWD

The most involving of public interactions is being in a pretty large crowd. This may be because the crowd is happy and you're mentally stimulated by what's going on. It may be as the crowd surrounds you and you're physically really stimulated by what's happening Whichever it is your body language will be affected not only externally but also internally, and you might react in a number of different ways.

If being with a lot of people delights you (as it does many people who have extrovert aspects), you may feel good inside. At a performance or sporting event, you may have bursts of adrenaline in your stomach or feel light-headed. This happens not only since the added input is stimulating all your senses but also because, when a lot of people get together, they begin to match one another on a really deep level. There is something especially satisfying about being in an audience and even a congregation where everybody leaps to their feet at the exact same time to praise.

But if, instead of getting excited, you become overloaded, then you can start to feel bad. Your body will indicate panic. You may feel ill and trembly. upset and aggressive. You might in the beginning lose energy and behave in a way that's more passive and compliant: we intuitively do this 50 as not to challenge the crowd. But if you still feel bad, then you are going to start to move in an uncoordinated way, changing color or breathing heavily as your body signals that it's under threat.

Alternatively, you may find yourself taking part the rhythm and deeply matching other individuals' nonverbal communication and, because of this, doing all kinds of things you would not usually do. If you begin to suffer any of the negative signs just pointed out, act instantly. Remove yourself from the circumstance, even if only for a little while; get far away from the movement and the noise. If you can't stop yelling and moving with the crowd and just stay still; hide your eyes and block your ears till things calm down.

Whether you have recently found romance or are trying to make a current relationship work out, words are often absolutely unimportant-it is what you do instead of what you say that counts.

This area of the book explores the subtle ways in which your non-verbal messages may make or break relationships. It defines the nonverbal communication signs that can initially bring you and a partner together how to signal interest and pair, and then how to develop your relationship sexually. It even looks at body language signs of feelings, describes some of the best ways that body language can help you determine and resolve problems, and shows you how to cope with the bad times. Finally, this chapter takes a look at the non-verbal signals of love, in all its stages.

Love at first sight So how does a person need to search in order to find love? It's a misconception that physical beauty is the crucial to finding love: it's not. Appealing women and men are, it is very true, more likely to receive attention; current research suggests that eye contact with a lovely or good-looking person actually really stimulates a specific satisfaction center in the brain. But people are drawn to personality as well as looks, so physical appearance is only one of the aspects associated with partner choice. Moeover, research has revealed that many people are wary of a person who is significantly more appealing than they are and are very likely to choose a long-lasting relationship with somebody of equal attractiveness.

So, what can be said about what appeals? In spite of accusations that men are more interested in woman's body than in anything else about her, research shows that both genders are at first attracted by a prospective partner's face. This makes a lot of sense: the face shows both vital personality and transitory state of mind. What brings in about it is normality. Recent studies have shown that the more a face approximates the mathematical norm in particular society, the more enticing it will be to other people. This propensity to prefer the standard is natural, with infants as young as 2 months old responding more positively to 'regular' deals with than uncommon ones.

Above and beyond this instinctive trend, there is evidence that women prefer guys' faces that look more 'adult,' while guys prefer women's faces look younger and more 'childlike.'

Whether we like this implication about men's and women's particular roles, a man with a strong jaw, chin and nose who gives off signals of being mature, reliable and able to secure may well appear more attractive to the opposite sex. Conversely, lady who shows infantile signals-baby signs like a little nose, high cheekbones and clear skin, which activate in all human beings a nurturing instinct-will appeal to a guy's protective instincts, a truth that might explain why smooth skin and pretty noses are usually the aim of women who have beauty treatments and cosmetic surgery. Remarkably, however, as women move more into dominant positions in society, 'adult' aspects like a pretty big nose or a firm chin are progressively viewed as feminine and attractive.

When it concerns the key facial function, the eyes, then in general the larger and paler the better-because of a basic human reflex. When we have an interest in something, the pupils of our eyes automatically dilate. The message this sends to the person we're looking at is that we find them attractive; they feel flattered, and in turn find us appealing. Big, pale eyes show dilation more undoubtedly, so they look both more brought in, and hence more appealing, to the opposite sex.

Coloring has an impact, as well. Lots of people are aroused by those with skins differently colored from their own, though the bulk form lasting collaborations with those from a comparable racial background. When it comes to hair color, the idea that blondes have more fun seems to be true, studies show that, in Western cultures at least, blonde women (consisting of 'out-of-the-bottle blondes) are thought by men to be more extroverted and bubbly though also less intelligent and less reliable as long-lasting partners. Brunettes are thought to be more serious smart and effective, while redheads are viewed as enthusiastic and moody.

Body appeal What brings in about a partner's body? Both males and females appear more smart and powerful if they're of medium height or above, that is, between 5 ft 4 in and 5 ft 8 in (16 and 1.7 m) for lady, and 5 ft 8 in and 6 feet (1.7 and 18 m) for a guy. A much taller woman can appear daunting; it's still true, even today, that all but the most positive of guys like to have their own physical stature stressed by contrast. Being smaller than about 5 feet 8 in (1.7 m) can be a romantic advantage for woman, though; as pointed out previously, a lot of guys feel drawn to and protective of women who look small and susceptible

A guy who is taller than average won't suffer the exact same issues as lady will, and in fact is most likely to prosper both romantically and expertly, because the non-verbal image he conveys is that of being confident and reliable. A little man, though, can be at a distinct disadvantage as his height gives the opposite impression. Research studies have shown that little men who do prosper in life or love can, though, be much more effective than their averagely sized equivalents-- they tend to develop more powerful personalities and increased social proficiency to make up for an unprepossessing appearance.

When it comes to shape, guys do assess woman on her figure, though less so than on her face, and the less so the older the man. As far as particular body parts are concerned, legs, butts and busts appear to be the regions that men most concentrate on; they're the body parts that mostly show gender difference and most reveal womanhood:

Women, conversely, will not judge a man's looks on his obvious gender signals nearly so much. Instead, she concentrates on his personality as displayed in face, eyes and nonverbal communication rather than on his broad shoulders or hairy chest. Penis size can do something in bed, (although women tend to prefer kindness in width instead of length), yet it has little or no bearing on preliminary attraction.

Weight-wise, slimness may not be almost as vital to beauty as the media tend to suggest. Women can see a well-rounded man as likely to be a great company, a protector or a psychological comforter, while only 31 per cent of guys in a recent study said that they preferred slim partners, and older men in particular have been revealed to like a body size that is in style terms, on the generous side.

However, if an individual's shape is verging on the XXL sizes, then they will come up against a general human bias against obesity-even kids have been revealed to discriminate against plump school good friends. The finaccurate) prejudice nowadays seems to be that while we have no power over our height or our color, we have the ability to manage our weight-- so, if we're not slim, that should mean that we are greedy and lazy

STYLE SENSE

Let's move from body inheritance, over which we have only minimal control, to outfits and image, over which we have a great deal. And here let's unmask yet another myth; overtly sexual clothes, such as tight denims or low necklines, aren't the way to find love. They are the way to produce stimulation in the opposite gender but relationships aren't built on arousal alone. A very sexually obvious fashion statement, for example, can put prospective partners off. And herein lies one of the primary differences in technique between men and women when judging a partner's attractiveness. For, although appearance counts for women, it often doesn't almost as much for men A lady's sense of style is, to her, a sign of status, intelligence and success. However, many a guy does not judge image or style in this light-he responds simply to how an outfit strikes his senses, not to the statement it makes. This is why he often chooses clothes that do not do him justice, and why he will typically compliment woman on her appearance when he actually doesn't think she looks good. What he sees is a particularly appealing color or texture, while what she's painfully aware of is that the style is three years out of date.

So if it is general image that attract a woman-be that a casual, sophisticated or hot image-- what attract a man when it concerns clothes? Color is important some men choose bright colors, others pastels, yet others prefer wealthy colors, dull colors or black and white. Men may also like contrast or noncontrast; the visual effect of two really different shades or the quieter declaration that is made by varying shades of a single color. They may prefer patterned or plain, glossy or matt, smooth or woolly, satiny or creamy, movement or absence of it, in both precious jewelry and outfits.

The issue here is that these variations don't necessarily indicate which sort of person prefers what type of image. There is a small preference among extroverts for bright colors, and a slight preference amongst introverts for dull ones, but beyond that studies have shown no real correspondence between a person's taste and their character.

Where this information is useful, though, is in observing the tastes of a specific person. If they always wear toned-down tweeds, then the chances are that sharp black and white will make them recoil: if they themselves choose clever business wear, they are going to probably choose a partner who dresses the exact same way.

There is a natural propensity for couples to match each other in all sorts of ways (see page 80) so, once you are in a relationship without compromising your own style, you might find yourself picking outfits that support your partner's likings. But remember, on the other hand, that the more involved with you a partner ends up being, the more they will start to concentrate on those parts of your body that reveal your character, ideas and emotions, and the less they will actually notice what you are wearing.

ATTRACTIVE SIGNALS

Recall, though, that though appearance has an impact, it is never as important as the more fluid aspects of body language. Within seconds of seeing you, a potential partner will be much less familiar with your appearances than your facial expression, your eye motions and your hand gestures. Within seconds of meeting a person who attracts you, you will be much less aware of his image than of the way he stands, moves or smiles.

So which body language styles attract? Confident nonverbal communication is certain to work. Even from across the room, somebody who moves quickly and with a smile, and who has an upright but relaxed posture, will be attractive-simply since onlookers will imagine that positive attitude being concentrated on them and so will want to make contact.

An equal assurance of attractiveness is a real interest in what is going on. Not many people, guys or women, can withstand the non-verbal message that broad eyes, a forward lean and authorizing nods send, even if these aren't being aimed straight at them.

Finally, openness signals are also efficient. For it is always an obstacle to make social contact, and making contact that may lead to sexual participation is much more challenging. So whatever you can do to make it easy for others to approach will encourage them toward you.

The standard standards for both genders are the same: let your body language show people that you are open and friendly, Keep your shoulders down, your gestures open your expression warm. Do not force yourself into a corner, with barriers up in the form of a bag or a chair, but make yourself available and quickly reached. Face

out into the room from where you are sitting and search for frequently as though wishing to make eye contact. In short, make anybody within variety feel that were they to approach you, you 'd welcome them.

Getting together

When it concerns making contact with a possible partner, it might all appear totally spontaneous But psychologists have determined a definite courting series that occurs in one form or another, in most situations where people want to check out relationship possibilities The first step is to show yourself off. Both men and women do this instinctively in any public circumstance, even when they're not searching for a partner. So once woman knows attention, she might begin with a general and unconscious show of womanhood, sitting up straight to stress her breasts or crossing her legs so that her ankles or thighs are seen to best benefit. She might make a screen of what she knows to be her own individual best functions, flicking her long hair back or turning her head to show her best side She may 'preen,' unconsciously improving her appearance by licking her lips, pulling her dress down and correcting the alignment of or changing fashion jewelry.

Across the room, a male rite will be going on. He will be aligning his back, squaring his shoulders, pulling in his stomach or adjusting his tie-the equivalent preening conduct for a man.

And, fascinatingly, once 2 people begin to display, Nature will provide a helping hand so that both undergo some automatic and unmanageable body changes to make you look more appealing, such as increased muscle tone, lowered under eye bagginess and partially fuller lips.

This traditional first stage of courting is not only about signaling 'I'm readily available, but also 'I'm safe' and I'm not going to mess you about.' So if you catch yourself deliberately showing in a general social situation, it's actually best to tone your movements down

POINTING If either gender then ends up being conscious of one specific person they want to attract, they are going to carry on to the 2nd stage of the courtship sequence, using directional pointers' to show that they recognize each other and that they're interested. Without purposely recognizing it, you will make certain that your gaze and your gestures are aimed in the other's direction.

If your interest isn't being returned, your interest will fade these nonverbal communication series naturally die if not reciprocated. If it is being returned, though, then you might well wind up being more obvious than you think. At this phase in the courtship sequence, once you've caught someone's eye, either side might be wary of getting it wrong, and so there's a natural propensity to exaggerate what you are doing to give unambiguous, non verbal encouragement.

So you might look to the other side, look till a potential partner returns your glance, hold eye contact for just a second, avert and then glance back to catch them still looking. To validate your interest. you may point your gestures, crossing your legs so that a knee or foot is aimed in the right direction, or make a gesture that suggests interest with your hand, finger, knife or fork. She or he, meanwhile, will be doing the exact same. You'll feel sure that they're interested, though unless you know nonverbal communication, you might not know why you make sure. If you see them doing all the things pointed out above, then you can be more certain that your instinct are well founded.

How easy it is to take the next step-making verbal contact-- will largely depend on the circumstance: how crowded the place, how near you are to one another and how acceptable it is to walk around and approach one another. If you're seated on opposite sides of a dining establishment, then you are going to need to work very hard to cross the divide, whereas in a club you really need only wait until the other person is dancing and then dance, also.

Once you have started to interact, then you will both be making a whole new level of assessments. Words will begin to matter more as you start to talk-though the topic of discussion will actually be irrelevant-you're sizing each other up and for that, body language is still crucial.

Initially, you're going to both be inspecting that what you saw from afar is just as good close up. Eyes, mouths and hands are the parts you will concentrate on most, aesthetically scanning quickly and nearly constantly with approximately two separate eye motions every second.

Equally, you are going to be having a look at each other's body rhythms. With good friends, the key is that your rhythms should match as closely as possible, but with potential lovers it may well be different rhythms that attract. So the other person might feel drawn to you since your easy body posture makes him or her feel comfortable, while you may feel attracted as their quick style gives you excitement. Although there needs to be an underlying matching maybe in your posture or intonation tone, your body rhythms might be complementary instead of similar.

Your sense of odor will also play its part. The closer you get, the more easily you're going to have the ability to pick up each other's personalized body odor signatures. If these do not appeal, then without your even knowing it, your body rhythms will become progressively mismatched; you're going to find it less simple to deal with one another and keep eye contact. If your smell signatures do appeal, though, the pheromones (chemical compounds developed to attract) that they contain will directly affect your nervous system, exciting and arousing you.

Finally, you are going to both keep examining one another's reactions. Is there shared preference: are you both readily available? Here, you need to take care. Studies show that all men automatically use non-verbal 'display' signals when with woman they prefer, even when they have partners, in simple fact even when those partners are in the same room.

FLIRTING

If the info you have gained by being close has made you both even more eager, you may carry on to the next step, which is to flirt. This part of the courtship series, which can last for months or even-in the case of some lucky couples-- for several years, bonds you together non-verbally by bringing you closer, encouraging you of the importance of the relationship, and guaranteeing that nobody else intrudes.

The opening move highlights all the signals of attraction. You move closer to each other, face each other fully look into each other's eyes and smile. You each find excuses to touch. emphasizing your words by a hand on his arm, or passing something across so your fingers meet. Your voices instinctively drop in pitch, be low, soft and husky as they would in love-making. The effect of being so near to one another makes your physical functions respond; you feel not only aroused but also lightheaded, as your heart rate arises and adrenalin pumps around your body.

The 2nd step is almost like a retreat, a withdrawal from interaction. For a short while, one of you will withdraw all the attention you've been giving: turning away to pick up a glass, responding to something in the distance, avoiding eye contact, masking your face or eyes behind your hand. The potential partner may react with a comparable withdrawal and, for just a second, you're going to both seem to lose the nearness you had, and your bodies might react with a burst of stress and anxiety, so that you connect for each other again with relief. It all helps convince you both non-verbally that this relationship is something you don't want to let go of.

And, just to make certain there's no risk to your relationship, one or both of you will also put up 'block off signals to discourage trespassers. When you first meet, it tends to be the man alone who gives these in an apparent, physical way, placing his body so that it effectively bars entry to any would be newbie. After several conferences, though, the woman will start obstructing. too, in more subtle ways, keeping the man's attention on her by her eye contact or laughter, a light touch or a kiss if at any time his eye is lured to roam.

The majority of these non-verbal flirting techniques are so natural that any mindful attempt at enhancement would ruin them. What you can do is to be aware of them and enjoy them-- they are instinctive ways of drawing in a mate, not unliberated manipulations. Your partner's external signals will show whether he or she is enjoying what is happening, and your own internal signs will tell you whether you are very happy with how things are progressing. Pull back a little if they're going too quick; encourage them with a smile if you like something they've done or said.

Through these non verbal strategies, you can keep each other included for sufficient time to evaluate the possibilities completely. If you aren't convinced, you will say your bye-byes and go. And if you think that the other isn't convinced-because you see their body position shifting their eye contact wavering and their gestures signifying that they have identified another person across the room-- then forfeit gracefully and turn your attention somewhere else

SEDUCTION

When both you and she or he is all set to move your relationship onto an intimate level, you are going to need to set the time and the place. Ensure you do so in a way that non-verbally as well as verbally develops the best chance of success

As far as timing is concerned, night is still probably the best time to start intimacy. Not only are people more available to intimate interaction when they have some time to relax at the end of a working day, but research has shown that increasing darkness encourages us to look and touch rather than speak. In one study of a group in a dark room, talking died away completely after about half an hour! So, cliched though it is the classic romantic place of a poorly lit dining establishment may best put your bodies in the mood

Choose a place where you're naturally positioned close together. Bodies are actually configured to make the leap from physical closeness to sexual intimacy. Once within the intimate distance zone of 18 in (46 cm), you're far more very likely to have sexual contact. And as this contact is also typically preceded by a spontaneous or 'excuse' touch, you may also want to choose a little restaurant table to make it more likely that you are going to unintentionally brush hands.

Choose a place that has music to make it more possible that your rhythms will enter synchrony, though not anywhere where there's audience participation-- you really want all attention focused inward to one another, not external to the room. In the exact same way, try to set up the setting for integrated block-offs as defined earlier on this page, for example, a pillar to shield you from other diners, or a table well away from the diversion of the kitchen door

Once the night's public activity is over, then-unless your partner feels uncomfortable from his or her own territory-it's best (and naturally, safest) to end up at your place. There you can plan the environment for availability plus reassurance. Make sure there's somewhere that you can comfortably sit together with the possible to move closer, though if your private space includes only a bed then make sure; it can feel too close to sex for comfort, and your bodies might develop compensatory barriers by becoming tense and careful

Throughout enable yourselves to move from the senses of sight and noise and on to the more sensuous channels of touch, smell and taste. So get rid of all diversions, like the phone or the roommates Introduce the standard components with a worthy reputation for boosting sex low lights, deep music, soft cushions. But again, do not exaggerate things with overtly sexual state of mind music or scene setting. If either of you feels unsafe, you will find it more difficult to become excited.

TAKING THE LEAD

Soon you're going to be ready for some serious touching. You'll most likely have touched before it's really uncommon to move straight from no contact straight to full sexual intimacy. You'll both have tested out the water with 'excuse' touches, and these will have shown encouraging: your smell, taste and feel will have appealed: you will both have progressed rather than back; your skin will have felt warm instead of cold to the touch. If all works out, at this moment your own instinctive nonverbal communication methods will take over

But what if you don't both spontaneously leap into one another's arms? Could it be that you are just not drawn in to each other? If either of you keeps demonstrating all the signs of a friendship, relieve back to the other end of the sofa and take things more slowly. If one of you is showing signs of diversion, such as pulling back, averting or attempting to talk instead of look-then quite just back off. If it's you who is distracted, then turn the illuminate and plainly and easily communicate that you do not want to take things farther.

What if your partner is returning all your display and flirtation signs, but things just aren't advancing the way you want? Maybe he or she watches out for going farther. Maybe you have misread the signs and your non-verbal interest hasn't truly been registered. You can take the effort in some ways. Though be alerted, these are not manipulative methods but forms of support. They are simply meant to speed up the natural procedure of physical intimacy, and if either of you is seriously withdrawn, none will work.

Move closer-as discussed before, being within the 18 in (45 cm) intimacy zone is a clear signal from you to your partner for vice versa) that you are really happy to make intimate contact. Increase the frequency of those accidental touches, which typically precede sexuality: look at something together so that you have to sit close together. When your hands do meet, make sure to communicate that the touch is not accidental, and that you are aroused by it

You'll already have seen the methods which the 2 of you are posturally or gesturally matching or mirroring one another. So, as you match posture, move a little closer. If the other person is attracted to you, you will motivate a response. As you mirror their gestures, allow your hand to linger, welcoming further touch. Lean well forward when gazing into their eyes, or raise your head when you snuggle up. Whisper something loving: they'll automatically lean closer to hear and, when your lips meet, it will be completely neutral to take things just that phase farther.

Emotional body language

Our human bodies are configured to have feelings, to signal-both internally and externally-when something wonderful happens and when something terrible happens. A love relationship will probably consist of both of these extremes of feeling.

It's fairly simple to identify when either you or your partner is overwhelmed with emotion, especially the 'timeless 6' emotions that have the same-body language all over the world, from Japan to Argentina: happiness, sadness, anger, disgust, surprise and worry. You'll signify happiness to each other through your smiles; unhappiness through your tears, anger through your raised voices or strong gestures. However, you may never ever see real fear in one another unless you're associated with a terrible event together).

Where real nonverbal communication skill emerges, however, is not in finding these obvious signs of feeling, but in noticing the much more subtle manifestations of feeling that everyone experiences every day Satisfaction, remorse, irritation distaste, confusion and stress and anxiety are toned-down versions of the full blown feelings. If you are able to identify the signs of these in yourself and your partner early on, you are going to be well geared up to manage them in you both.

The first sign of an emotion you might well notice in yourself will be some type of internal rush of energy. This is since feelings were originally developed as a way of resourcing you to cope with an outdoors hazard, as well as signifying to others in your tribe' that you needed aid with whatever was impacting you.

Feelings are real physical events, just like appetite or thirst, with your whole autonomic nervous system moving into action. On the inside, adrenalin pours into your bloodstream your heart beat and blood pressure skyrocket, your breathing rate rises, your nervous system is flooded with sugar to give you energy. your digestion system decreases so as not to squander that energy and your coagulation rate arises in case there's blood spilled.

Parallel to this, each specific feeling will have its own particular influence within your body. Anxiety may make itself felt by a churning in your stomach that is so typical that it has a special word in English-' butterflies.' You may also get tightness down the centerline of your body, a faster heartbeat, a dry mouth, a slightly cold experience and maybe an unexpected need to go to the toilet. If you are experiencing remorse, you're going to feel your eyes prickle, a vague precursor of tears, your nose or throat may feel partially blocked, and there'll typically be a heavy feeling down your center line. The earliest indication of inflammation may be a sudden tingling, a movement in your stomach, a rushing in your head or hands, an abrupt clenching of your jaw.

Know your emotions as you feel them day by day. That way, not only do you acquire more communication with your own body, actually motivating it to tell you when it thinks there is something to be cautious of or mad about, but you also have more chance of responding to your feelings, which is a skill beneficial not only in love relationships but also throughout your life.

HIS EMOTIONS AND FEELINGS

A Unique note here on guys' feelings. It's usually difficult to read a man's psychological body language. Traditionally, men in our society aren't motivated to be in touch with their emotions. The most frequently showed male emotion is anger and that's often the one they reveal in order to alleviate the internal stress of all the physical events described above. (Extremely usually, in fact, their real, underlying feeling may be one of sorrow or fear).

A nervous man will have normal frowning concern lines on his forehead (in apes, this signals a desire to leave from something but not having the ability to). His shoulders may be raised, as though in defense, and he might tend to hunch forward rather than sitting typically. He'll usually bite his lip or move his mouth-almost as though he's attempting to talk through the issue in his head.

And, while men typically find it hard to weep, a guy who is feeling regretful or sad may well show redness or puffiness around the eyes, with a gleam of wetness along the lower eyelid. His mouth will shiver partially, his body slump and, without really knowing that he's doing so, he may sigh greatly.

An annoyed man, on the other hand, will tend to gaze with lowered brows, just as if staring down an opponent before an attack. His nose may flare, his lips tighten, his shoulders stoop, his motions get brief and sharp or uncoordinated. His color might change, so that his face turns white or red, as his nerve system alternately makes him mad and then tries to relax him down.

However, what if he's experiencing conflicting feelings mad at his partner but afraid of her reaction: resentful that she went out but relieved that she's back? It's vital for lady to spot signs of such inconsistent feelings, as if she doesn't she might deal with things in the wrong way, reacting to the single emotion she thinks she sees instead of to the other feeling that the man is also feeling.

So both women and men really need to watch out for conflicting signals. These signals normally occur in zones, with one emotion appearing in one zone while a completely different response happens in another. Researchers speculate that this happens as different parts of the brain are advising different parts of the body. Normal contradiction zones' are: top half of body versus bottom half (for instance, tears on the face but inflamed foot taps); top half of face versus bottom half (smile to reassure you, but fear in his eyes); left half of body versus right half (tilting head or moving shoulders and hands), whole body versus single gesture (a relaxed posture and caring expression plus clenched fist). And, naturally, don't forget to look for body language that actually opposes the words a tranquil statement but a mad mouth, a loving phrase but a withdrawn hand.

The boss yells, the train is late or on a more serious level, you lose your job or a member of the family dies. Whether it's you that's feeling bad or it's your partner, you might feel that the most valuable and caring way to behave is to be pleasant and encourage him or her to be the exact same.

Nevertheless, from a body language point of view, the reverse is often true. For when we continuously lower our feelings, we put our bodies in a double bind. If we constantly feel miserable, anxious or irritated-- and then, as a result, constantly put the brakes on these emotions-our natural control mechanisms will go into overdrive, and the result can be to keep our bodies on a seesaw of stress. Medical research now suggests that this sort of emotional suppression can result in all kinds of long-term problems, including heart disease, cancer and depression. So rather than keeping a stiff upper lip, a more useful and effective way of handling your body reactions might well be to ventilate the emotion, therefore letting your body off the hook.

How can you best do this? Check this out with one another, for needs differ between people, and people want different types of support. But if either of you is anxious or miserable, then often an entire body cuddle is the best way to offer comfort-it reminds your body non-verbally of when you were extremely little and absolutely secured, and so makes you feel safe and loved. Hold each other securely, closely and without any effort at sexuality, feeling your breathing and heart-rates start to match reassuringly.

If either of you is upset, then exercise usually helps, by utilizing up the adrenalin that the body produces Running can be good: hitting a cushion can feel better. Make your movements strong and powerful and breathe gradually while you move. If your home is soundproof, don't be afraid to shout while you're doing it if it isn't, bury your head in the cushions to shriek. If you can, flail or shout in helpful unison; but if it's each other you're feeling bad about, do all the above by yourselves, and meet up only when you feel better. (And whatever the source of the anger, if the emotion keeps returning, look for outside help).

Once you sense that you have uttered all your feelings, and you are spontaneously beginning to feel better, use the following non-verbal series to key back into regular life. Get to your feet and move, with your head up and eyes somewhat raised to the ceiling, Breathe deeply and slowly Do some sort of complex but non-risky physical activity such as wiggling your toes one by one, which will allow the nerve system to start using some of its energy. Then do some sort of complex but undemanding mental activity, such as counting the ceiling tiles, which will turn your attention from any residual psychological signals you might be experiencing.

This sequence can also work if you really need to act naturally when you're feeling bad. It will help if you have no opportunity to express your feeling and will carry you through until you can deal with the problem appropriately. But like all the suggestions in this section, it isn't the resolution to deep emotional trauma, serious relationship conflict or long-term depression, for which you really need ongoing support or expert therapy.

When problems hit your relationship, the answer in a lot of cases involves the application of words. You talk through problems you discuss them with others or you check out a therapist and talk to him or her about them where body language helps is, first, by signaling you to an issue and, second, by making certain that the words are most effective. And, just sometimes, there are body language solutions to your issues.

What can you do if, for instance, you suspect your partner might be tricking you? His/her nonverbal communication won't tell you precisely what the lie might be or what the truth is, but it can help you clarify whether there's an issue.

Partners who are lying don't want to show what they actually feel their initial tactic may be naturally to reduce their non-verbal signals. So lock initially for 'blanking signs'- being quieter and somehow more still than normal, with gestures and expressions softened, less eyebrow flashes and a tense mouth and jaw as they keep control.

Or they might show you a false front, with a caring expression. But check the smile. A genuine one is balanced, one side of the face to the other, with wrinkles around the eyes, an incorrect one is asymmetrical, stronger on the left side of the face (in right-handed people), with no eye wrinkles and a fixed, gradually fading expression. If they're attempting to stop themselves telling you something, they may stutter, trip over their words, use the choker' gesture with their hand to their throat, or talk through their fingers just as if attempting to block off their voice.

To see behind this masking conduct, look at those parts of their body that they have less power over than the face or hands. You may find 'leave' movements of legs or feet, stress in the shoulders or stomach. They might non-verbally comfort themselves, by touching their face, smoothing their hair or 'wringing their hands. Their breathing may be unequal, with little stops and jerks, their skin color may change and they might perspire and blink more than normal.

So what can you do? You can never get a partner to tell you what they do not want to, but a simple body language technique can make it clear to you both that something is being hidden if you want to challenge them, do so in personal and when you're close. Position yourself so that your partner has to face you directly lean forward and hold their hands to stop the worried motions that provide release from inner stress. Look into their eyes, which will make it challenging for them to manage their feelings. Make your voice soft instead of mad, which will stop them from hiding their guilty nonverbal communication under resentful nonverbal signals.

If they squirm and wriggle, if they can't meet your eyes and if all their anxious nonverbal communication signals increase, then there is an issue, and that fact will be clear to both of you-though how you then deal with things is up to you. If, on the other hand, your partner stays calm, unwinds into your gaze and sighs, then they may simply be a supremely good liar. The chances are, however, that your concerns are truly for nothing.

Any suspicion of trickery instantly ends up being more upsetting if you suspect that your partner is deceiving you about an affair. How can you tell and what if anything can you do about that?

If the possible 'other woman' or 'other man' isn't part of your circle, then in all sincerity an intelligent partner can usually hide this secret effectively. The regular non-verbal signals like a new fragrance lingering in the vehicle or love bites on the neck are so commonplace that your partner and his or her lover will keep away from them thoroughly

What should signal your suspicions, though, is any change in a partner's non-verbal method toward you. And that surprisingly enough holds true whether the change is for the better or for the even worse. For instance, an abrupt and unexplained drop in the amount you see your partner is bad news. However, it may not be entirely good news if there is a sudden increase in the amount you make love-it might mean that your partner's sex drive has been stimulated by a new lover, arousing a desire for more sex in general, including from you. If you're in a long-lasting relationship then watch out for an unexpected drop in your bonding signals, like eye contact and forward leans. But also understand the introduction of any new non-verbal series, like taking your arm rather than holding your hand, or cuddling up on the couch or in bed in a way that is different from typical. While your partner might well have the ability to stop telling you about a new affair, it will be far more challenging to stop the new bonding habits they're learning with their lover from sneaking into their collection with you.

If you think that your rival is a person from your circle of friends, you do have more chance to learn the truth since you can watch them together. If an affair is just building and has not started yet, you may see all the regular display signals from your partner-grooming habits, display habits and flirting. If your suspected competing reacts, then you do have a cause to worry.

If you think that an affair has already started, watch, too, for an absence of connecting intimately between your partner and your competitor. Be as suspicious of that as you would be of increased rapport-for if the stops taking a look at 'her' stops smiling at her, eliminates all expression from his voice when he talks with her and keeps a greater distance between them than he would have before, then he has something he needs to hide. Check such an uncommon shift in behavior by looking at your partner's unconscious signals, if postural matching and unconscious 'directional tips' of hand, knee and shoulder are still directed toward you, then there might well not be an issue. If, though, your partner's non-verbal signals are all directed at the possible new lover, the time has most likely come for you to stop observing and begin acting-challenging your partner, talking through the problems and creating a circumstance in which words and gestures are both focused solely and truly on you.

PUTTING THE BRAKES ON

At the start of a relationship or at any given time throughout it, you may feel the need to slow things down sexually or emotionally. Your partner wants to go farther, to sleep with you or to marry you want to stop and take your time

The problem is that in that kind of situation, it is exceptionally tempting just to 'be good to your partner.' This simple fact often makes women, in specific, use nonverbal communication that appears far more pleasant and concur than they feel inside. So even when they do they typically accompany it with a comforting half-smile or head nod, as though to say. It's all right.' Regrettably, the message a partner might get is, if you keep asking, eventually I'll say yes.'

The key to keeping away from this type of misunderstanding is assertive nonverbal communication. If you feel that you are being pressed into something, begin by breaking any physical contact and moving back slightly so you're not lured to weaken your message by a caring pat or an unexpected clutch Face your partner directly and look him in the eye-a sign that you truly mean what you are saying. And to make your non-verbal communication even clearer, unwind by taking a deep breath and letting it go slowly

Don't smile, even partially, as this is the one body signal that weakens a 'No' more than any other. Instead, let your mouth fall into an unwinded but serious position, and drop your chin just partially so that your throat is open and your voice will not sound 'little-girlish.' Swallow, so that when you do speak you don't begin with a doubt or stutter and after that talk gradually and quickly State what you want to say, and then stop. (Assertiveness instructors usually advise that for maximum efficiency, you decide what your message is in just several words and after that, if pressured, just repeat this message rather than including any descriptions or certifications).

This style of nonverbal communication won't give you a totally easy flight, as nevertheless calmly you present your case, you are rejecting your partner what he wants, and he is going to frown at that. But this method will keep away from the unlimited rounds of conversation and argument that can often happen because he hopes that your negative answer is really a positive one in disguise.

What if the reverse is going on and your partner is just saying no to you? How should you react? First, if they actually use the word 'no' then, whatever their body language, accept what they are saying just as you would really want them to if you said it. Disregard body signs; they might well be signifying apology, placation, quilt or fear, all of which will confuse the message.

However, what if your partner says yes and you suspect they mean no? Check carefully for methods which their body is truly signifying an unfavorable to you like minute shakes of the head or wagging of the fingers. Notice doubts in speech, swallowed phrases or incorrect starts that suggest that what they want to say is something really different from what they're actually saying. Reading the real meaning on both verbal and non-verbal channels may not eliminate conflict, but it will make communication clearer and, in the long run, create a better resolution.

It's over now

You might think that if you feel nerve-wrackingly anxious when your partner phones, or furious when you see them, your relationship is in deep trouble. Even more so, though it certainly is bad news, it might not be the worst. For if feeling is still there, then you still have an emotional bond: your body still considers this relationship to be important. The relationship might be an unpleasant one, but it is not over.

On the other hand, if what you experience when you phone or meet them is simply a minor sinking feeling or an anesthetized sensation, then your body might be telling you that this relationship now has no significance in your life. It may well be time to move away.

If you still feel something, but your collaboration is having problems, check out your shared nonverbal communication. A long-term relationship may not show the in-love signs of a new one, so don't worry if these signs aren't there. Do worry, though, if your partner moves back as you progress or vice versa, if you can no longer meet each other's eyes, if you are mismatching and tripping over one another in words and motions. All this means that you are no longer in non-verbal synchrony.

Next, check the energy level between you. A practical relationship will create vitality (except in cases of short-term fatigue), giving your motions vigor and your voice tone strength. If, when you're around each other your energy level drops totally, your posture and gestures are tired and dropped and your faces and voices without expression, then there is little stimulus left in your collaboration.

Check, too, those most fundamental of emotional barometers: taste and smell. In a dying relationship, you usually suddenly find that these are unpleasant. You might think that your partner has all of a sudden developed halitosis, when the simple fact is that their body odor signature hasn't changed, it just does not attract you any more.

Lastly, have a look at your sexuality. A drop in the frequency you make love is natural in a long-lasting relationship, and may also happen temporarily if either of you is under tension. But a distaste for love-making, a diminishing from touch or an absence of sexual response, even once you start. is your body's way of telling you that there's absolutely something wrong.

Can nonverbal communication assistance to reverse the process? Most of the signals pointed out above are symptoms of a hidden problem, not triggers. They reflect the simple fact that you and your partner have incompatible objectives, that you have lost faith in each other and that you have ended up being thinking about other people. So attempting to change the body language will not work, though if you're able to talk things through and fix them, then, as if by magic your non-verbal signs will become positive again. The one exemption to this is where your problems are because of physical incompatibility. You really want more cuddles, he does not: he wants the sex this way you want it that other way. In this circumstance, particularly if you get the help of a certified therapist, you can work to straighten your nonverbal communication, both in bed and out of it.

What if you decide to split up? Then, the struggle between you will mainly be in words the settlement of the break up, the discussion of who gets what. But once the final decision is made, you can reduce the split by guaranteeing that you don't give out unhelpful non-verbal signals. When you have to meet, try to avoid communicating your inflammation with tense shoulders, a constant frown, tight lips, confrontational eye contact or a sharp voice. Confronted with these signals, the human body intuitively moves into attack mode and you're going to find your partner becoming significantly hostile to you, so do your best to keep calm.

On the other hand, if you offer too many positive signals, you're going to give the non-verbal impression that you're interested again. So ensure that when you meet you keep enough distance between you. Erect barriers-a dining establishment table or a workplace desk-- and if you sit down, choose a chair that has arms. Make a clear no-go location around you with your gestures, your absence of eye contact, and with a slight frown if your partner techniques. Provide the clear message that you want to be on your own and you will avoid any unhappy attempts at reconciliation.

If you are fortunate, then your sexuality will be based on real affection, and your commitment will be based on love.

It may appear just as if what we in the Western world call 'love' has absolutely nothing to do with the body's conduct. Definitely it's all pure emotion-or, more cynically, nothing more than a fairy tale dream? In fact, current research has revealed that the phenomenon is based on real physiological responses that the body makes to meeting and bonding with another person. When you first set eyes on somebody and there's an instant attraction, your entire body responds. Your brain releases a chemical called phenylethylamine. This has the same impact on your nerve system as any powerful addicting compound-- you get high. You become increasingly knowledgeable about your own body and its stimulation, you are in a state of constant desire. You might lose your cravings, be not able to sleep, suffer adrenaline bursts that make you restless and absent-minded and have an irregular heartbeat and high blood pressure. These results are not all in your mind; they actually exist, they truly impact your body. they actually are activated by your loved one and they actually are there so as to bring you together.

How you handle these signs depends totally on your circumstance. If you're both free and able to fall in love, then you can follow your instincts. You can start creating a bond with your partner in all the incredibly romantic ways in which are so common of falling in love. Expect to be a little scatterbrained, to have lots of energy to feel extremely good; your brain is drip-feeding your body the love drug, and as long as that lasts, you're going to feel different.

But what if you or the person you really love can't form a reciprocal relationship, or having formed one, can't make it work? Then what you experience can be extremely painful, as your body is suffering an overdose and there seems to be no other way of easing the symptoms. The most beneficial way to approach this problem actually has nothing to do with nonverbal communication or with non-verbal communication-it is to be disillusioned with your desired partner as rapidly as you can, by whatever means you can Then, your brain will naturally stop producing phenylethylamine. After several weeks or months of withdrawal signs and convalescence,' where you feel tired and weepy, you will wake up one day feeling normal again.

Remaining in love if your relationship develops, then after a few weeks or several months, your body will notice that there is now no longer any real need to push you towards a steady relationship. A new set of chemicals is released into your brain, this time enkephalins, which help you overlook troubles and literally weaken any strong pain you may feel. You start to feel calm inside, as though sedated -as certainly, to some level, you are. Your appetite returns, and you begin sleeping again. You feel energetic but not frenetic-relaxed and happy.

Your relationship is most likely going well. If you have a battle or suffer some disillusionment with your partner, you can handle this possibility as the enkephalins help you do so. As in the first stage of friendship (see page 40), you are learning all about each other, verbally and nonverbally. You still feel sexual, but not as urgently. so though you still have sex, you are not desperate if you do not.

Your natural non-verbal bonding system is working well-- and here's the threat. For it is really simple while you're in this stage to make a commitment based on how you feel rather than on actual compatibility. Success here lies in the ability to overthrow your body language in this situation, it might be deceptive. Instead, analyze such hard-headed us as underlying beliefs, common attitudes and life goals. Only if these things fit should you make any commitment.

Reinforcing love If your relationship continues, then at some point-and this could be anywhere from several months to several years after you've at first met- a 3rd chemical change in your brain occurs. The enkephalins continue to allow you to deal with any difficulties, but contributed to them is a dosage of endorphins, that make you feel intense pleasure and long-lasting satisfaction.

Inside, you feel peaceful, relaxed and satisfied. And your non-verbal communication with your partner is telling you that all is well with the relationship. You may, of course, deal with the occasional issue, but you can still cope with it. And as a result you have the ability to start turning your attention out to other regions of your life re-establishing contact with friends, raising your kids or building your career.

Seen from the outside your relationship begins to look more like a friendship than a sexual relationship. The first signals of sexual intimacy. the eye contact, touch and block-offs that signalled 'Keep clear, we're busy to other individuals are irrelevant now, you don't really need them for reassurance, and other people don't really need them so as to know that you're a couple.

You'll be matching, though, on levels deeper than any but the most intimate friendships. You'll not only be matching posture, mirroring gestures, showing voice tones and phrases and using up the same breathing and heart-rate rhythms, you will also have developed your own non-verbal customs. These are little series of conduct that are specific to you-ways of gazing, ways of turn-taking, ways of kissing, even ways of fighting that only you 2 do together. Through all this matching, you might even have developed similar physical weaknesses or vulnerabilities: a lot of couples tend to die of the same illness. Non-verbally, your nonverbal communication will look to an outsider like a dance without words.

Remaining in love

What if all of this does not happen the way you want it to happen? The bottom line is that if a relationship does not encourage this sort of deep-level communication in time, then it might well come to an end. And, as has been stressed earlier, using nonverbal communication to help an ailing relationship or to reinforce a dying one is usually attempting to do insufficient, too late.

What is actually true, though, is that you can use those nonverbal communication methods to maintain your love and Protect your relationship. From the start, keep one eye and one ear on your matching sequences. and provide opportunities to develop them. Do things together that require you to learn what one another's nonverbal communication patterns are, such as playing a sport, or making love, which is the ultimate matching activity. Work so that you become mindful of your own and your partner's non-verbal codes, both in bed and out of it, and continuously improve your recognition and comprehension of these codes.

Ultimately, if all matches your relationship, and your mutual life helps you to comprehend each other more on a mental level and support each other more on a psychological level, then your nonverbal communication will do the same.

Whatever your profession goals, body language will help you prosper in them. As well as examining your qualifications, experience and efficiency, people will, usually unconsciously, be judging you on other factors-whether you appear non-verbally positive, qualified and efficient.

The nonverbal communication of the workplace

This area of the book explores work situations: dress code and how best to play the system, how to use body language to feel proficient at work, and the methods which nonverbal communication can help you cope both with your associates and with your superiors. It then goes on to look at 3 particular work scenarios-- the meeting, the customer and the interview. And finally this part of the book demonstrates how, as you continue up the profession ladder, body language can help you fulfil your potential and accomplish your objectives.

Making an impression

What you wear at work makes an individual declaration about you. It could be a way of saying to your boss that you're prepared for promotion or to your associates, that you're a friendly person; it could be an assertion to a client that you know what you are talking about. So it's smart to think about your agenda and choose your outfits accordingly-and, for woman, that includes your devices, makeup and hairdo too.

Is it crucial, for example, for you to be seen to have power and authority, maybe since you want to influence a customer or be taken seriously as a freelancer? The days of power-shoulders are over, but the fact still remains that if they want to appear powerful, both genders need to adopt some of the non-verbal icons of masculinity. For women, the key depend on shape and color, detecting the partially customized look that is reminiscent of a guy's suit, in collaborated clothing, using dark or toned-down shades, with light makeup and a basic hairstyle without too many womanly curls.

Say, on the other hand, that you want to create a cooperative, rapportful relationship at work -perhaps because your job includes a bargain of one-to-one interaction or assistance. Then you really need to choose outfits that reflect more womanly emblems-such as lighter, brighter colors, patterned rather than plain materials, and unstructured shapes that signal relaxation and an accepting nature Women can also use makeup to emphasize those parts of the face that are most expressive-- eyes and lips: but keep the colors softened so as not to move over the boundary between womanhood and sexuality.

STYLE STATEMENTS

You might need to look knowledgeable in your job since the product and services you're handling has a professional' or scientific image. Pick up here on the icons of the occupations who dress completely in black or white. Black says 'know-how and intellectualism' because it's related to the church and the law, while white says 'wisdom and empathy' because it's associated with medicine-which is why some cosmetics counters dress their assistants in white uniforms. To support the non-verbal message being offered, women might really need to soft-pedal their gender signs so regarding appear expertly nonsexual. Tie hair back off the face and choose small, easy accessories and a natural or unnoticeable makeup

All these agendas-power, rapport, sexuality and knowledge-- will probably blend and match in whatever work you do. You will want to appear powerful but approachable, knowledgeable CRACKING THE GOWN CODE

Overlaying your personal style decisions, you will also need to take into consideration the basic unwritten dress code of your company. This is a sort of home style that is created by the employers, who laid down an official code (no denims ... tie your hair back ...) that is then refined by employees who adapt it informally to suit themselves (we all wear black here ..). Learn the code and follow it, unless you want to give the non-verbal message to your managers that you do not care, and to your associates that you're not part of the team.

The official code will be simple to follow. If the office supervisor or workers department do not know about it, it doesn't exist-o ask. However, there are no written guidelines to an informal gown code-- you will have to work it out for yourself. It will differ not only within occupations but also according to the company you work for, which department you work in, which age band you belong to and what level of seniority you hold. And it might be just as threatening to your associates if you dress above your level as it will be to the management if you dress too casually for work. One very obvious example is that there are some jobs, like training or middle management, where the gown code is still to wear a firm suit all the time. But conversely there are some, like fashion journalism or PA, where you need to dress 'now' or you are doomed.

The secret of following the unwritten gown code is to take a look at the following rigorously for your department and your level. What type of outfits do people wear? How formal or casual are they, how stylish, and in what colors? How many new attires do people wear over time, and is it acceptable to wear the same thing two days running? What kind of shoes are used? How much jewelry, and how expensive and outrageous is it? What hairdos do people normally choose, how long do they wear their hair, and is it colored? What makeup, if any, is worn? As part of your effort to be successful in any new job, make a psychological note for the first few days of all these details, until you begin to comprehend the secret code-- and only then head out and begin restocking your closet.

FEELING PROFICIENT AT WORK

It is essential to be in a great emotional state while you are at work. If your body language signals 'moody,' then coworkers will start thinking of you as that sort of person. And that sort of person may well be passed over for promotion.

Some recent research from sports psychology suggests that there is a short-term solution to this problem, and that you can use non-verbal techniques to change your state of mind. Using these strategies will make your nonverbal communication change spontaneously and truly, for a while, at any rate, you will neither feel in a bad state of mind nor show it non-verbally.

Have you ever noticed your self-confidence slipping before that huge meeting or during that crucial presentation signs of non-confidence are simply a way of silently signifying to others that you feel you can't handle a scenario. Before words were first spoken, people called for help by utilizing panic signs. Now we use a toned-down version of those same signs unstable gestures, a shivering voice, speech stutters, a dry mouth, a pale color and bad coordination. If your uncertainty is not well established - if you know your stuff but just do not have self-belief-then you should try the following strategy.

Start by thinking about an event when you were confident, when you just knew you were able to do something well and you did. Imagine yourself at that time, seeing what you saw, hearing what you heard, sensing what you picked up. This psychological exercise acts as a kind of physiological pump primer, reminding your body of how it feels to be confident. And as you begin to remember completely, you're going to probably sense yourself reacting, unwinding, starting to breathe progressively and starting to focus

As you connect with this feeling, overemphasize it just a little. Stand as firmly as you can, perhaps with feet somewhat apart to stable you. Hold your head high, maybe even tilted back partially. Breathe deeply and relax even more as you do so. Be aware of your heart rate slowing imagine your adrenalin waning and feel your mouth being more and more moist again. You may want to bite your tongue to encourage saliva; relax your singing cables to give your voice a lower and more confident quality: say something aloud or count from one to 10 just to get rid of any remaining vocal squeaks or trembles.

You'll really need to practice feeling positive in this way to train your body into reacting confidently when you really need it to. Once you know you can summon up the state purposely, then give yourself an aide-mémoire by contributing to your routine a little movement, like a deep breath or 'stand straight' action. Then, when you are not confident and really need to be so, use that same movement to trigger the positive mood and fully remind yourself of the nonverbal communication you really need to adopt.

One caution, though: This pointer is only beneficial when you're actually proficient but, just for a minute, you have forgotten that simple fact. Do not push yourself to use confident nonverbal communication when, in reality, you should be nervous-when you're underprepared for a project, for instance, or just not skilled enough to handle the situation. If you truly can't perform and you know it, your only solution is to enhance. If you ask your body to come up with the products in this circumstance, it will simply and quite justifiably refuse.

INCREASING MOTIVATION

Whereas the nonverbal communication of confidence is really all about being relaxed and steady, the body language of inspiration is about being alert and energetic. Of course, continuous demotivation at work is the type of circumstance that needs profession therapy, not nonverbal communication. But if you need to get to the end of a boring training course, or rake through the last half hour of a tiresome meeting, then you can persuade your body to offer you with vitality, in much the same way as you convinced it to offer you with self-confidence.

You know it when you're encouraged. Your adrenalin is running high and you are energetic Many people see you looking diligently, listening alertly, your whole posture upright constant and focused, your motions fast and certain. So if you find yourself doing just the opposite-leaning back, dropping, hiding a yawn, de focusing-then you need to get moving and get your energy going It's no coincidence that Japanese firms often integrate in exercise for staff as an important part of their working day).

Begin by making a reason to leave the room, pleading a need to go to the bathroom if necessary, once alone, begin moving around. It may look foolish beginning your shoes and jumping up and down in your business suit, but you're going to look a whole lot more foolish losing the contract. The aim is to keep going, maybe not till you are sweating a lot, but certainly till you have significantly raised your heart-rate. You can also use the old trick of dabbing icy water on your wrists and the back of your neck to get the blood flowing.

As soon as you're back in the room or the training course, use the same sort of strategy to achieve the body language of inspiration as you did for the body language of confidence. Recall the last time you felt inspired. Replicate those signals, leaning forward in your seat, drawing your legs back under you just as if you are interested and keeping your breathing silent but fast.

If you practice feeling driven, you can add to your collection the ability to be inspired almost on command. And you can develop a trigger of determined nonverbal communication comparable to your trigger of confident body language- gesture such as clenching your fist or clicking your fingers that will remind you of your energetic state and enable you to reproduce it when you really need to.

SURVIVING TENSIONS.

You probably know when you feel stressed out. Your stomach churns, and your heart pounds. If you feel like this constantly, you need a long-term program of stress management, which motivates you to change your entire life style But if you just periodically get overwhelmed, then nonverbal communication techniques can help.

When you feel stressed-perhaps just because of some sudden trigger such as bad news about some project, or perhaps just because of tension developed during the day-then start by going somewhere where there are no disturbances. This may mean closing your office door firmly and taking the phone off the hook. Sit comfortably, or perhaps rest on the floor if you can and, then just for 5 minutes, let go totally.

You may find it helps to think of a time when you were relaxed or to daydream about somewhere where you could relax: an isle in the sun, a nation walk, a warm bath. Enable your whole body to relax: if it helps, concentrate on each part independently from your feet up through your legs to your hips, stomach and upper chest. right across your shoulders, down to your arms and hands and back up to your neck and head. Breathe deeply all the while, counting slowly from one to ten as you do so.

Then lie quietly for just several minutes, concentrating on your breathing before counting backward from ten to one and slowly coming back to the here-and-now. Adopt this relaxation series as part of your day-to-day routine where you can, but also, fix it in your mind as a memo to your body. Given enough practice, just counting from one to ten gradually will activate your body into relaxing sometimes when you don't have the opportunity to carry out the whole series.

The 3 methods in this area will not give you deep personal change or resolve all your problems. But if you want to complete the job without despairing, make it all the way through the meeting without falling asleep. or make it to the end of the day without shouting, then these body language repairs' will do the trick.

Dealing with associates What makes work situations so challenging is the fact that, with people thrown together day after day in close distance, office politics develop: alliances, hostilities, power-plays. You need to understand these to be able to handle them-but as they are going to hardly ever get discussed without predisposition, your only real source of insight may be the nonverbal communication around you.

Start by evaluating the existing pecking order. We're not talking here about official systems of supervisor and staff, but about informal hierarchies between you and your associates, the clearly defined order of importance in which everybody has their place. What dictates this will depend totally on what's valued within your particular group: seniority or rank, a greater wage, being married, being skilled, being fashionable-or even being male.

To discover just where you are in your group pecking order, observe. The higher in the order you are, the more people will listen to you. If you Say something others lower in the pecking order will pay attention, though people higher than you will feel able to disrupt. The higher you are, the more people will agree with you, nod when you are talking, take up on your ideas. Men, incidentally typically interrupt in a 'high pecking order' way, whether they're officially your remarkable or not. I a male colleague does this constantly, woman needs to eliminate back, or the non-verbal impression she'll give will be that she accepts her 'low chain of command' role.

WHOSE SIDE ARE YOU ON?

And also checking for a pecking order, watch out for alliances and hostilities Basic friendship will be extremely clear, spot the traditional signs of people hanging out together and moring than happy to deal with one another, have lengthy eye contact and 'match' and 'mirror.' When friendship spreads throughout a whole group or department, search for group tie signs like a propensity to wear the same sort of clothes and go to the exact same spots for a beverage after work, and also territorial signs, like always commandeering the exact same table in the cafeteria.

If you want to be part of an alliance, then follow the standards that are put down on pages 35-6 for making friends. The fact that you are working in close proximity will help to reduce significantly the initiation time: the deep-level body matching that you develop while doing the same sort of job often means that you fall into natural consistency. You can also improve this procedure by using the guidelines that are given in the areas of this book on rapport, reading minds and comprehending personality. However, keep in mind that work alliances, built up day after day, year after year, are more territorial and protective than even the most permanent friendship groups. So be prepared to sit silently in the break for quite a while, to laugh together with the jokes for a long time and to go to the preferred wine bar after work for quite a while before you're accepted as one of the crowd.

If you aren't accepted by coworkers at your place of work-through jealousy, maybe, competition or simply as you do not fit in for some reason that may be difficult to see since it's not acceptable to be honestly hostile in a scenario where you need to collaborate every day. If things are inexplicably going badly for you, then watch out for what are called 'leakages.' where an enjoyable expression is all of a sudden disrupted by a micro clue of a more negative emotion.

Men will show leaks of anger more than women, who usually show heat or regret more easily. So, if you are successful on a project. and you turn to find somebody else's congratulatory smile fleetingly spoiled by a mouth movement of the sort that can only be called bitter, what you're seeing is envy. If your efficiency is being compared with somebody else's, and that person's face for a short while becomes tense and aggressive, what you're watching is competition. If you tell a joke and amidst the laughter you find the occasional mocking eye raised skyward, then what you are seeing is hostility. Forewarned is certainly forearmed.

If you do see any of these things, then it will be hard to work with those people. So you're going to actually need to change things. If it's a group that is really against you don't try to tackle them together, they will take their non-verbal lead from one another and close ranks. Instead, divide and dominate; if you face an enemy on her for his) own, she for he) will be a lot easier to deal with. Attempt discussing a project together on a one-to-one basis, and use all your rapport skills to make your 2 sets of body language fit until you are matching and turn-taking easily. If you do this, then the quiet message will be neither 'I'm against you ...' nor "You're getting to me ... rather it will be 'We're similar and I want us to get on well together. Without actually knowing why your foe will automatically feel slightly better about you. And, similarly automatically, as you match her or him more, you will begin to feel more considerate towards that person. Because of fundamental physiology and life conditioning, you will find it harder to match male associates than female ones. Nevertheless, if you use this technique regularly and with everyone with whom you have arguments, you will gradually, with time, notice that they feel less antagonistic towards you, and that you feel more friendly toward them.

Lastly, what about sexual attraction in the office? You can tell who's brought in to whom by watching their display behaviors - though you will not get precisely the same signals in the office as you would in social circumstances. It will all be reduced just because of the context, and woman in particular will not be nearly as obvious in her flirting signs since she knows that people are watching her. When courtship develops into a relationship, though, the positions are often reversed. She might feel more safe and secure and will start to let her feelings show, he might be less apparent now that he has attained his objective. So you can often tell that romance is now on the program when she begins looking at him, and he stops looking at her. This is especially true if he's married and is having an affair; if both of them are wed, then overnight, they might both start neglecting each other completely.

If it's you yourself who is having a workplace romance and want to hide it, then you need to keep your body language friendly instead of all of a sudden either passionate or hostile-both of which are immediate giveaways. Instead, remember how you used to relate before you became included and behave easily. Ensure that your nonverbal communication signals friendly coworker' instead of 'enthusiastic lover. Check the distance you stand from each other good friends are comfortable at between 18 and 4 ft (5 and 1.2 m) apart, lovers are very happy to move closer-while secret lovers sit on opposite sides of the room. Monitor the amount of eye contact you have; good friends are really happy to avert, lovers look, secret lovers never ever even glance. Know the intonation you take with each other good friends keep a normal voice tone, lovers let their tone drop and decrease, secret lovers hardly speak at all.

Handling your boss Whether you work straight for a boss or just report to one, you really need to handle her, or him, efficiently. Start by identifying, broadly, what style of management she, or he, follows so that you can react appropriately. 3 typically acknowledged. Some styles are 'autocratic' 'democratic and laissez-faire.' An employer can significant in one or have elements of all three, and each style can carry with it a particular nonverbal communication technique. If your body language complements your boss's management style, then you will have a problem completely free relationship. If your non-verbal techniques are opposed, then you may have problems.

The 'autocratic' boss-who is traditionally likely to be a guy-- values the non-verbal signs of status that come with the job the desk, the nameplate, the company automobile. So he may reinforce that status with his nonverbal communication, dressing expensively and officially. He'll probably use a typical 'leader's posture with straight back, squared shoulders, controlled motions, head held high. He will keep barriers between you, closing his door, sitting behind his desk, making certain by his expressionless face and unemotional voice that you do not get too friendly. He'll gaze you down if you start to get out of line, and will let his displeasure show in his expression and tone. Women who play the autocratic boss can be criticized as 'inhuman.'

If you want to be the best staff member, never try to undermine that official body language. Treat him formally, knocking when you get in, waiting to be told to sit down, Extremely different is the 'democratic leader traditionally more likely to be female. What is necessary to her is the people side of the job, so she'll use nonverbal communication to build individual relationships. She'll arrange her office for optimum access, with a chair near hers, or an informal 'social' location for meetings. She'll generally adopt sociable nonverbal communication, with a positive expression and clear signals of rapport; she'll tell you something instead of write it down, and will more than happy to come into your office instead of make you go to hers. She'll typically touch you, as a gesture of assistance or congratulation. By the way. men who adopt democratic leader body language can be misinterpreted as being over-friendly.

To succeed with this kind of boss, you need to tread a careful line. Just choose her open door policy, whether you are at ease with it or not, and match her rapport with friendly non-verbal signals of your own-relaxed motions, smiling and voice tone. But do not think that she wants you to act as a peer and begin disrupting or talking over her rather, aim for 'customized rapport, where you act in a friendly way, but still always wait for her lead in speaking or acting.

The 'laissez-faire' boss keeps clear, letting you do your job in your way. More guys are likely to adopt this method. This type of boss might be an introvert who has got a promo through skill instead of through people skills. So he might establish barriers-to keep his stimulation levels down-while not remaining in the least status-conscious. And he may be rather friendly, but do not have expression and eye contact as he doesn't want to get involved. He keeps his range, often being away from the office, communicating through memos or hardly examining you at all.

Here, your body language needs to stress self-sufficiency, Act in a more equal way, matching him and holding eye contact in a way that assures him that you can cope Show the nonverbal signs of inspiration, so that he knows you will do the job. But don't expect high levels of interaction; keep conferences short, sit at an angle from him so he doesn't feel invaded, expect him to avert or appear distracted. Anticipate to be left alone for long periods and when he does come back, give him a report that shows by your body language that you're independent, positive and efficient.

READING THE SIGNS

Having actually established your boss's general patterns of behavior, it's a very good idea to examine much more specifically what his/her nonverbal communication signs mean in specific circumstances.

Maybe the most fundamental thing you will want to really know is whether your boss is in a tiff. As it often isn't acceptable to show this at work, he or she might not tell you but it will display in other and a propensity to treat items violently, slamming down phones or closing doors with a bang.

Also learn the signs of whether your boss is busy or friendly. A closed door is the official indication, but even if it's open, he or she might be using subtle 'leave me alone' signals, such as a shoulder or arm obstructing your technique from the door, raised shoulders to eliminate noise, a head bent over the desk. Surprisingly, the opposite signals-lean back in the chair, look out of the window, and a defocused, nontransparent gaze and, for a man, feet on the desk - don't always mean that it's OKAY for you to interrupt. These might be signs of remaining in downtime see pages 44-5). In this case, your boss might actually not be almost as interruptible as when relatively making notes, but is in simple fact alert to what is happening outside, eyes scanning the room, ears punctured' to overhear conversations.

Next, learn the signals your boss uses to direct interactions with you. They'll be discreetly different from those of discussion, since you both have a job to do, and since your boss supervises and you are following instructions. She or he may direct the discussion, with a deliberate pause and head movement requiring a response from you, a look and raised eyebrows to check if you have comprehended something. A circling hand gesture might mean it's time to proceed to another point. while eye contact and a nod may mean that a guideline has been completed. At the end of an interaction, when your boss wants to be alone, she or he might shuffle documents, shift in his/her chair or tap both hands on the arms as if to get up and get on. At this moment, a male boss will tend to be more direct, taking a look at his watch or getting up from his chair to suggest the end of the meeting.

Finally, it's useful to know, even several seconds ahead of time, if an employer going to say yes or no to something. Here, micro-movements come into their own; usually, as somebody thinks about a proposition they show with these subtle shifts just what their response is. Watch carefully, and you'll see the micro-nod for yes-- or the much more subtle blink that shows the head nod and also marks key phrases with which somebody agrees. Conversely, see the micro-shake for no, or a parallel negating movement of a finger. If your boss is still uncertain about something she or he might give an 'not sure signal, most undoubtedly an up-and-down shift of the shoulders, a 'balancing' movement of the hands or a wiggle of the lips.

Naturally, each boss will have her or his own unique set of non-verbal codes. So you'll need to check out not only all the above body language series but also any others that are crucial for your boss, and then tailor your reaction to them.

Strategies for conferences Despite the simple fact that an organization meeting is officially about discussion, it's the underlying nonverbal communication that makes or breaks it. So look at where you will hold the meeting. What's your aim? A conference room might have big tables and status icons that will make the meeting formal and professional, but holding it in any type of social area with a sofa and coffee table will help build good relationships. If you allow people into a private office environment, the fact that it is on your territory will put you more in control, while using a neutral meeting room may make it easier to create cooperative teamwork.

Next, look at seating for conversation and group-building a table where everybody can sit in a circle or side by side is best. For cohesion, choose a smaller table that will make participants feel closer in both senses of the term for imagination allow space to expand. If there's very likely to be an one-upmanship and you want to increase it, put people on opposite sides of the table, if you want to decrease it, put them on the same side. Put whoever is controlling the meeting at the head or at the middle of the long side of a crowded table; an individual you want to keep under control might be positioned alone on the long side of the table, opposite more than someone.

Also look at how you are going to welcome people as they show up. There are subtle non-verbal messages in every technique of welcome. Meeting participants at the elevator and escorting them to the conference room makes some feel reputable, while to allow a friendly, long standing client to come up unescorted may give him or her the message, 'You are among us.' Keeping individuals waiting in the foyer till the precise time of the meeting can give the impression that you're busy and crucial, while inviting them up beforehand for a pre-meeting coffee might suggest they're friends

Recall all that is been said about greeting methods, letting your method tend towards the official as being more suitable for the work context-a handshake, for instance, is seen in the business framework as showing your effectiveness and skills. But also be flexible; greetings vary according to four aspects: the society of the company, your status compared with that of the person you're welcoming, the length of time you've understood them and just how long since you last saw them. In some professions, you lose kudos for not kissing the most rare of contacts on both cheeks in others, such conduct even with long-term associates is out of place.

HIDDEN AGENDA

Whatever's on the official agenda, watch out, closely, for the individuals' real intentions. The American psychologist David McClelland has determined three kinds of business goal:

' affiliation' an agenda for group cohesion and good feeling: accomplishment,' an agenda about getting the task done; 'power,' an agenda of remaining in control. Each has its own particular nonverbal communication pattern.

An affiliator-typically a lady or a sociable man-will most likely show up early to welcome people and speak with them. She will want to call everybody, and might actually trigger a delay in the meeting, as she is so busy 'touching down. She'll normally sit where she can see everyone and ensure they're included, and her nonverbal communication will show this, with a lot of eye contact, smiles and turn-giving. She'll show signs of tension if there's a dispute, and will just use a soothing voice and hand motions to appease people and reconcile them. She may stay behind afterward, chatting.

An achiever will tend to arrive strictly on time: she or he will not want to squander a minute of the day. If he does speak with anyone in advance, it will typically be someone essential; he is going to often choose to sit next to that person at the table, or alternatively, next to somebody who might block the project and needs to be persuaded. At the meeting, this task-oriented person will have the right equipment, note pad and pen, appropriate papers. He'll want to keep a strict agenda, will calmly hear everyone out as long as they're speaking relevantly, but will get irritated at what he considers 'waffle. He'll relax once crucial decisions have been made, and might then leave early to go on to another meeting.

A person who wants power at a meeting-typically a man or high-flying woman-may arrive just partially late (a normal power-play) to make a point or to get a movement passed, so you need to wait for him. If he does arrive in time to socialize, he is going to typically spend the most time with those who are also in power, like the chairperson. He'll generally try to sit in the power position'- the head or short side of the table or in the middle of a long side if he wants to affect a ton of people. During the meeting, he will tend to talk loudly and rapidly and will disrupt if things aren't going his way. He'll stay right to the end, in case something happens when he's not there, but once the prominent people have left, he will leave too

Many people have one of these basic agenda patterns in most conferences they participate in, though they can change agendas on particular occasions. But, equally, many will integrate the 3 patterns, aiming for a little of each. Display agendas-in other individuals and also in yourself because they will not always refer what people say they really want from a meeting and you may need to be alerted of this beforehand. Also, once you have identified what agendas people have, you can use them all to help you achieve an effective meeting letting the cohesion individuals develop a good group feeling beforehand, then utilizing the task and power individuals' reactions during the meeting as your mine detectors for whether things are on course and what power plays are currently in operation.

A conference is a group conversation, so if you are chairing it, you're going to really need all your regular conversational abilities, but with the added challenge of needing to direct the group toward a contract.

Begin by indicating your leadership at the start. Use your confidence trigger (see pages 85-7) if you really need to, then sit high and straight and take a look around, holding eye contact with everyone and waiting till they're quiet before beginning Throughout, keep taking a look at everyone-a message that you're still in charge. Remember that, if you remain in a mainly male environment, psychological openness can be seen as ineffectiveness, so control your facial expression and stay away from demonstrating obvious anger or distress.

One of your primary tasks will be to demonstrate to people when they can speak. Keep an eye out for signs that they really want to-normal turn-seeking behaviors, yet aimed not at the person who's talking, but at you as chairperson. So as well as keeping one ear on the speaker, you also have to look for intakes of breath, for inflamed finger-tapping, for those who are attempting to get eye contact with you, for those who are signaling 'my turn' with a finger lift or a minute wave of a pen. When you do give an individual consent to speak, clarify this with a stressed turn-giving wave of the hand in their direction, to show everybody who now has the floor. Provide the speaker your attention by turning to them and taking a look at them, which will encourage others to do the same.

Silencing people may be more difficult than getting them to speak. You may have to use the more difficult methods that you use in discussion, and if these do not work, say their name (a word the majority of people will respond to, though immersed they are) together with a frown to show that there's an issue, You can also use a 'silence signal-- there are universally recognized ones, such as tapping on a glass or with a gavel.

During the meeting, you may also really need to guide people towards agreement or defuse dispute when contract appears far. So constantly check individuals' feelings by means of their body language. Keep in mind those who appear uninvolved, revealed by a small lean back, stretched-out legs, and a hand supporting the head. Re-involve these people by asking a question or welcoming a comment. Also note from the body matching, where alliances are being formed and broken during the meeting, if someone is changing sides, for instance, their body language will indicate this beforehand as they 'match' or 'mirror' the person they're now allied to even before their words show that they have moved their viewpoint.

What if there is trouble? Watch open for 'deceit' signals as once a person begins to lie, other participants really typically sense it and begin to get inflamed or upset. And whether or not anyone is lying, if you can hear voices rising and see upset expressions, then even if what is being said, appears safe, make sure. It's sensible, at this moment, to require silence and enable a cooling off period while you talk for a few moment, to enable irritation to die away.

At the end of every meeting, make certain that decisions have been consented to non-verbally and also verbally. Look at each participant in turn and check their contract signals, watching for eye contact, uncrossed arms, mitro nads of the head or 'it's done' signals like closing a laptop or folder and pushing from the table. If instead you get a hostile posture, crossed arms and frowning or out of balance facial expression, micro-shakes of the head or a shift of the shoulders, you need to return and re-discuss or re-confirm the product. If you struggle to do this, participants may-whatever they say at the time-mis-remember what was discussed, or misunderstand what was agreed.

You and the client If you handle the public, in a retail or business setting you need to adopt an entirely different style of nonverbal communication from typical.

The non-verbal message in any service circumstance should be, I am here to help'- so nonverbal communication needs to be alert and inspired. But the message isn't Tm your good friend,' so normal social signals usually really need to be toned down: you might smile but not too commonly technique close but not too closely. give eye contact but not in a challenging way.

At the exact same time as being valuable, you also have to supervise. Because you are accountable to the company you work for, you have to use the body language of respectful assertiveness, your posture confident, your movements sure, your eye contact direct. As you're going to be meeting the client or customer for only a short time, you have to show them the ropes with bigger than-life gestures to make sure they know what to do quickly and easily.